MOUNTAIN SKIING

MOUNTAIN SKIING

Vic Bein

THE MOUNTAINEERS/SEATTLE

THE MOUNTAINEERS: Organized 1906
". . . to explore, study, preserve, and enjoy
the natural beauty of the Northwest."

First printing March 1982, second printing December 1983, third
printing January 1985, fourth printing October 1986

Published by The Mountaineers
306 2nd Ave. W., Seattle, Washington 98119

Published simultaneously in Canada by Douglas & McIntyre, Ltd.
1615 Venables Street, Vancouver, British Columbia V5L 2H1

Published simultaneously in United Kingdom by Cordee
3a DeMontfort St., Leicester LE1 7HD

Book design by Marge Mueller
Illustrations by Judy Swedberg
Photographs by Vic Bein unless otherwise credited

Photographs on pages 60, 62, 64, 70, 74, 75, 83, 85, 86, 88, 92, 101, 102, 103,
104, 107, 108, 109, 114 by Tim McClure

Unidentified photos—
Cover: Author doing telemark wedeln in the Rockies in May. (Photo by
Naomi Yager)
Title page: Fox Glacier, New Zealand
Page 8: Mt. Ruapehu, New Zealand
Page 19: Looking for a campsite in British Columbia, Canada
Page 119: Using a self-timed camera, the author demonstrates the delights of
steep skiing in the safe corn snow of June. Mt. Baldy, Colorado
Page 137: Home, snow home—Mt. Ruapehu, New Zealand

Manufactured in the United States of America

Library of Congress Cataloging in Publication Data
Bein, Vic.
    Mountain skiing.

    Bibliography: p.
    Includes index.
    1. Cross-country skiing.   2. Cross-country
skiing—Equipment and supplies.   I. Title.
GV855.3.B44   1982   796.93'028   81-22290
ISBN 0-89886-034-2   AACR2

*To all the friends who have made this book possible
and to my parents*

Contents

Page

Preface 9
Acknowledgments 11
Introduction 13

PART I: NORDIC MOUNTAIN TOURING 19

   1 Nordic Ski Equipment 20
   2 Ski Tuning 44
   3 Uphill—Waxes, Skins, and Wedges 47
   4 Onward and Upward 52
   5 The Turn—Unweighting Methods 61
   6 The Turn—Basic Techniques 66
   7 The Turn—Advanced Techniques 81
   8 "Let's Boogie" 95
   9 Falling 108

PART II: ALPINE SKI TOURING 119

  10 Alpine Touring Equipment 120
  11 Extreme Skiing 128

PART III: THE MOUNTAIN ENVIRONMENT 137

  12 Personal Equipment 138
  13 Camp and Community Equipment 148
  14 Sleds 155
  15 Shelter 159
  16 Avalanches 168
  17 Hypothermia and other Emergencies 175
  18 Wilderness Ethics 181

Appendices 185
Index 189

I look to the mountains;
where will my help come from?
My help will come from the LORD,
who made heaven and earth.

Psalm 121: 1-2

Preface

While still a teenager training to become a proficient Alpine skier and cross-country (X-C) racer, something great happened to me. I was skiing back home from a X-C race and, seeing a shortcut, left the track. Little did I dream that such an insignificant decision could change my whole life and my philosophy of skiing.

The shortcut led to a spectacular cliff, where the view of the mountains in the sunset was more gorgeous than I ever knew existed. The sunset was only an appetizer. Next I discovered a gentle bowl with scattered trees and the snow glistening pink in the last sunrays. The powder was fantastic, and I decided to try a few turns. Having never done so before on wooden X-C boards, I was delighted to discover how gracefully they cut S's through the fluff. That and the tranquility of the wilderness really turned me on to skiing the unbeaten tracks. Since that happy day many things have changed, but backcountry skiing is still my way of life.

Similar experiences are capturing more and more people every year. As "yo-yo" skiing (Alpine skiing on packed, lift-served slopes) becomes more overcrowded and expensive, Nordic touring is increasingly a sought-after alternative. Once on skinny boards, you are free of the ski lifts and can go wherever your wildest dreams dictate, totally free in a peaceful, unpolluted, almost unreal world.

Even a Sunday X-C "stroll" in quiet woods is an unforgettable adventure. But I am particularly attracted by all those beautiful chutes, the magnificent bowls, and heavenly powder in the mountains. More and more people are discovering these things and finding them to be the ultimate ski experience.

The idea of mountain backcountry skiing is by no means new. It simply means going up to the mountains to enjoy their tranquility, challenges, and often the best powder on earth. It is the healthiest way to get to the top of ski runs that will make you dizzy with their beauty. It is the challenge of storms, avalanches, and the steep.

My aim is to present a book on mountain backcountry skiing, but one which is different from existing books. First, I want to make skiers aware of the great but underestimated potential of Nordic equipment which many find suitable for even the most demanding backcountry skiing. Second, I would like to discuss many aspects of Alpine touring. Third, I have tried to write a book interesting to beginners, as well as the better-than-advanced skiers. But since there are many good books about the basic aspects of backcountry skiing, I prefer not to repeat their content and write yet another primer. Instead, I strongly encourage you to study the books listed in Appendix B. I have tried to emphasize little known but important subjects in this book, for example, Nordic ski design and how it affects turning. For the most part, I have avoided making recommendations on specific brands of equipment because new products become available so frequently. It's better for you to talk with other skiers and to ski shop sales people when you're ready to make a purchase. I do, however, tell you what *features* to look for in the equipment you purchase.

Throughout, I emphasize the simplest, purest forms of skiing. This is not a manual of ski mountaineering or climbing; little is said on the use of ropes or crampons. The name of this game is skiing — on the level, up and down — as simply and with as few technical gadgets as possible.

Acknowledgments

I'd like to express deep appreciation to the following for their help with this book: John Pollock for his interest and encouragement; Ann Cleeland for her editorial supervision; Donna DeShazo for her production coordination; Marge Mueller for her photo sequences and book design; Judy Swedberg for her illustrations; Ray Smutek and Molly Killingsworth for editing; Patricia Silver for proofing; Paul Ramer for his advice and assistance on ski technology; Naomi Yager and Tim McClure for their help with the photography; and Dr. Stephen Bezruchka, for his suggestions on the hypothermia and frostbite sections. Without their help, this book would not have been possible.

Snowgum trees on the way to Mt. Kosciusko, the highest peak in the Australian Alps.

Introduction

Until quite recently not many people would consider Nordic skis for much more than racing or Sunday tours near home. "Vic, you'll kill yourself on those skinny boards" was the usual comment of friends seeing me taking off down some 45° chute. They, of course, couldn't imagine doing that kind of extreme skiing on anything but Alpine skis with heavy and rigid bindings and boots.

Obviously, the potential of Nordic gear is greatly underestimated. On the other hand, composing theories about tackling ice or other very difficult situations on skinny skis is of course too ambitious. The range of skiable conditions is quite a bit narrower with Nordic touring gear than with Alpine touring gear.

Still, I am convinced that on 95 percent of all mountain backcountry trips, skiers would do just fine on Nordic, rather than Alpine, touring skis. Why then do 3-pin skiers so often have problems on steep terrain? Because one or both of two essential requirements are often missing: 1) correct technique, and 2) proper ski equipment.

Nordic skiers are often reluctant to take instruction; many rely too heavily on techniques acquired on rigid Alpine equipment. These attitudes usually lead to bad habits and prevent the development of fine technique.

Proper equipment is immensely important in Nordic backcountry skiing. Everybody knows that turning a 210 cm pair of Alpine skis in "mashed potatoes" snow is not the easiest. But Nordic touring skis of the same *excessive* length are still popular among backcountry skiers. And an improperly designed ski will not allow anyone to fully utilize turning techniques, no matter how good a skier he is.

Turning on Nordic touring skis can often be easier than on Alpine touring skis, as surprising as this statement may sound. This is because Nordic skis weigh much less and have a lower *swing weight*. (Swing weight, the torque needed to pivot a ski around its middle, acts as a measure of the ski's resistance to rotation. The longer and heavier the ski, and the more its weight lies in the extremities, the higher the swing weight. Although skis with high swing weight are stable at high speeds, they are difficult to turn.) A Nordic skier feels his skis much better, almost as if he were skiing on bare feet, because he does not wear rigid boots.

But the limits of skiable terrain are reached much sooner with Nordic than with Alpine touring gear. Powder and corn snow are the best for Nordics. Ice, breakable crust, and very steep slopes are the worst and should be left alone for safety's sake. Although gear is important, the Nordic skier has to rely also on finesse and technique. I consider this a challenge, and meeting it is rewarding and thrilling.

On the other hand, there are almost no limits with Alpine gear, as extreme skiers, "skiers of the impossible," prove all the time. And because of the rigidity of Alpine equipment, a skier can often get by with improper technique, unless he encounters unusually difficult conditions.

What equipment is best for mountain touring? Once a skier understands the advantages, disadvantages, and limits of both Alpine touring and Nordic touring, the choice shouldn't be difficult. I am a strong advocate of Nordic touring and know that its limits are far beyond what most people think. But on some occasions I switch to Alpine touring gear to be able to negotiate icy slopes or very steep couloirs (gullies) with full enjoyment and more safety.

Weather and terrain are often the deciding factors. The coastal ranges of Norway, New Zealand, and North America are icy most of the winter, and they are consistently steep. Those mountains require mountaineering skills and heavy gear. Yet spring and summer turn the snow to corn, and skiing becomes so easy it can even be done on X-C racing skis.

One year I went with a group on a ski trip to Mt. Ruapehu, 2797 m, a magnificent dormant volcano in New Zealand. Being late spring (November), the snow cover varied between rock-hard ice and soft, delightful corn snow. The only way to get to the upper glacier was with crampons. Skins or klisters—nothing would work that icy

Heavy rain changed powder to glare ice on Mueller's Peak in Australia's Snowy Mountains.

morning. Some of us even wished we had brought Alpine touring gear. Later when the snow softened, we all were swearing by our Nordic gear.

The crampons were put to further use that trip. They were invaluable for ascending ridges to find steep skiable slopes. And on the last day, we wouldn't have been able to go down to the road at all if not for the crampons, their points giving the only support on the steep ice. Skiing was out of the question.

Such a story is luckily uncommon. Nordic skiers can usually find soft snow, if they look around. In some instances, though, there is no way but to grab ice axe, crampons, and Alpine touring gear, as most skiers usually do in the New Zealand Alps, where the average snow is definitely not Rocky Mountain fluff.

So there is no clear-cut, universal choice. I suggest trying out the "skinnies" first. If you don't fall in love with them, or if you reach your limits with them, then move on to the "bigger brother"—Alpine touring.

COMPARISON OF SKI TOURING EQUIPMENT

Nordic Mountain	Alpine Touring
SKIS	
Visually similar to other types of Nordic skis, but built much stronger and wider. May include metal edges and other Alpine ski features.	Very similar to ordinary Alpine skis for lift skiing. Specially designed for a wide variety of difficult snow and terrain. Almost as light as some Nordic skis.
BOOTS	
Heavier and stiffer than Nordic trail skiing and racing boots, but much lighter than Alpine boots. They resemble ordinary walking boots. Expedition-type Nordic boots, which can also be used for climbing with or without crampons, or overboots are necessary for very cold conditions. Comfortable.	Ordinary climbing boots, Alpine ski boots, or preferably, specialized ski-mountaineering boots. Often used for climbing on foot with or without crampons. Expensive, heavy, and very rigid. Uncomfortable on long trips. Mostly waterproof and very warm, but sweaty.

Nordic Mountain   Alpine Touring

Nordic Mountain	Alpine Touring
BINDINGS	
Standard, 3-pin Nordic Norm* touring bindings. Very simple construction, hence reliable and easy to repair. No release features, but the free heel can be considered as offering quasi-release. Sometimes the boot may be jerked out of the binding in a fall.	Similar to Alpine bindings but with the added feature of a free heel climbing mode. Most offer full release features. Many parts and sophisticated design make them more vulnerable to breakage and malfunction. Expensive and heavy.
TRACTION	
Conventional cross-country waxes. May also be fitted with climbing skins. Some models of skis have built-in traction devices.	Removable, synthetic fur "seal skins" affixed to the bottom of the ski. Cross-country waxes may be used under some conditions.
WEIGHT	
Around 4 kg total	Around 10 kg total
COST	
Approximately $250	Approximately $500

*Nordic Norm is an international boot/binding standard.

I.

nordic mountain touring

1. NORDIC SKI EQUIPMENT

Skiing is an activity that is totally dependent on equipment. Swimming or running require no equipment, and there are many other enjoyable pastimes for which equipment requirements are minimal. Not so with skiing. Skis, poles, boots, bindings—all are essential. Perhaps more important, the equipment must be coordinated with the task at hand; it has to match the *kind* of skiing you intend to do.

With Alpine gear, the choices are relatively simple. However, with Nordic gear, the situation is much more complex. There are many distinct forms of Nordic skiing—track skiing, cross-country touring, racing, mountain skiing—and each has its own specific equipment needs.

Let's begin by reviewing the basics of equipment for Nordic-style mountain skiing.

Boots

Boots are the foundation of a mountain touring outfit, and only a boot sturdy enough for mountain touring should be considered. Shoes designed for X-C racing, boots which come with low cost "package" deals, and most rental boots are totally inadequate.

A good pair of Nordic boots should be ankle height or above, torsionally rigid, and light. The uppers should be made of high quality, double tanned, full grain leather. A one-piece upper construction, with a minimum of stitching, reduces the chances of water penetrating through the seams and damaging the seams by abrasion. The leather should not be waterproofed with plastic. The best soles are stitched to the uppers by a method called a Norwegian welt construction.

Trying to save money on boots is not a good idea. An extra $20 or $40 can often assure you of excellent quality, good torsional stiffness, and long wear. A boot that can be twisted lengthwise like a dish rag is not even worth looking at.

Heavy lined boots dry very slowly in the backcountry. Light ones, after becoming wet, virtually dry out on your feet on a warm, sunny day. One time a snow bridge collapsed and I found myself water skiing in a creek for a few minutes before being able to scramble out. My gaiters and overboots didn't allow much water in, so my light boots dried out quickly.

If you want to combine skiing with easy climbing, you'll need heavier boots with mountaineering lug soles. For extreme cold, consider double boots with removable felt liners. However, the simpler, less expensive, and lighter boots can give sufficient turning control, especially when

Double boot with lug sole, for extreme cold

used with heel locators (discussed later in this chapter). Some skiers want as stiff a boot as possible for telemark races and resort to even such extremes as ski jumping boots, often costing more than the fanciest Nordic touring outfit. Another, much less expensive alternative is to buy a pair of old lace-up leather, double Alpine ski boots from a ski swap or secondhand store, and get a shoemaker to replace the rigid soles with softer ones that bend at the ball of the foot.

Many boots do not come with binding toe plates, but you can add your own. I like the plates with six mounting screw holes, and prefer to use 1 cm or longer screws. Before mounting toe plates, make sure the boot is properly aligned over the center of the ski and fits tightly in the binding. If necessary, grind the sole down. Then press the bail down and make a pin impression in the sole. Drill the three small holes for the pins. Align the toe plate over the holes, and outline it. Cut out that area carefully, so the plate will be flush with the sole. Finally, mount the plate with the six screws, and use epoxy for a secure bond.

Fine boots deserve a good wax-base waterproofing treatment, but first, while they are "oven fresh" from the shop, coat the exposed stitches in the front of the boot with a glue-like seam and welt treatment to protect against cutting by the binding bail. Then apply the waterproofing to sun-warmed boots. If you use a hair dryer or other source of heat for warming, be very careful not to subject the boots to temperatures hotter than your skin can tolerate. Accordingly, don't expose them to an excessively hot sun.

I believe traditional leather-and-stitch boot technology is now reaching its maximum state-of-the-art level, and truly revolutionary improvements are no longer possible. Although tremendous progress is being made in ski technology (fiberglass and other space-age materials, P-tex bases), boot design lags behind. Soon, however, there may be Nordic backcountry boots made totally of plastic, with carefully programed stiffness and flex characteristics allowing for more extreme skiing.

Gaiters and Overboots

Many Nordic skiers come home from their first trip with cold feet, wet trouser legs, soggy socks, and damp boots.

Some even get frostbitten toes. These problems can easily be prevented by wearing gaiters and overboots.

Gaiters should extend to the knee, not just to the calf as some do, and must be wide enough to accommodate your thickest legwear. (Long pants are much better than knickers.) A good gaiter has an elastic cord with a toggle on the top. The bottom also has an elastic cord, a front hook for attaching it to the overboot, and a toggled cord going under the boot to ensure a tight closure and to prevent the gaiter from being pushed up by deep snow.

While overboots may not be necessary for plastic Alpine touring boots, they are *essential* for leather boots, especially for light touring boots. Overboots protect the leather, keep it dry, and make single boots almost as warm as double boots, with the extra advantage of a system that is

Waterproof fabric

Gaiter and overboot

light and versatile. Even an uninsulated overboot made of a single layer of tightly woven fabric increases foot warmth dramatically. The well-designed models extend above the boot and envelope it completely, and the soles are made of a heavy-duty, abrasion-resistant, waterproof fabric.

The use of zippers (which may break) and of Velcro fasteners (which may ice up) is debatable. I prefer to make my own gaiters, simple tubes with a toggled drawstring on the top, elastic along the bottom edge, and an instep drawstring.

Over Nordic boots wear overboots which extend well above the ankle. They should be insulated for the coldest climates. They too can be very easily made at home. The fabric for the uppers of gaiters and overboots should be breathable, but strong and tightly woven, such as Gore-Tex 60/40, or uncoated pack cloth. For the soles a waterproof, abrasion-resistant fabric works better.

Skis

It seems as though present designers are trying to squeeze both Nordic and Alpine design features into a pair of Nordic backcountry skis. Unfortunately a union between such conflicting requirements doesn't produce good results. It is like trying to marry a Rolls-Royce with an earth mover.

A mountain ski will be used primarily on untouched snow, very seldom on prepared tracks; hence it has no great need for features important to a track-running ski. The most exciting aspect of a backcountry trip is the downhill run at the end, preferably through untouched powder or corn snow, but just as likely through breakable

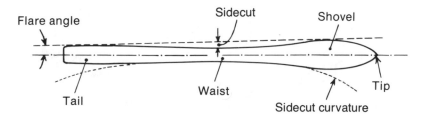

Anatomy of a Nordic ski

crust and heavy snow. Hence, mountain skis should be easy to turn, which is to say, they should be designed similar to Alpine skis, which are for nothing but turning.

Nordic Ski Design

How do some ski design features relate to turning? In Alpine skis, the midsection (the waist) is narrower than the tip and the tail. This produces an arc along the edge, called *sidecut* or *side camber*. Most X-C racing skis have no such sidecut, but a so-called parallel or even a negative sidecut; either the ski sides are parallel or the waist is the widest part.

Camber, the upward arc of the middle of the ski, is another design feature. In an Alpine ski, it distributes the weight of the skier equally over the entire length. When the ski is pressed down by a skier's weight and centrifugal force in a turn, it bends into a variable curve, called *reverse camber*. The more flexible the ski, the easier it is to press it into a reverse camber.

When a ski is edged and pressed down, it assumes an arced curve, the result of the interaction between the sidecut and the reverse camber. This curve is used for turning. The closer the skier follows this curve, the more he is said to be *carving*. In other words, a ski carves if its tail follows exactly in the tip's track, leaving only a narrow "carved" path. This path will be defined by the geometry

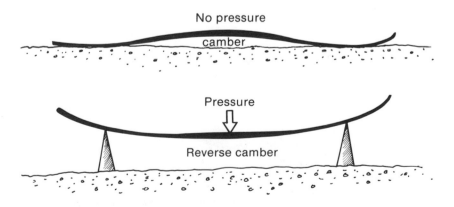

Ski camber and reverse camber

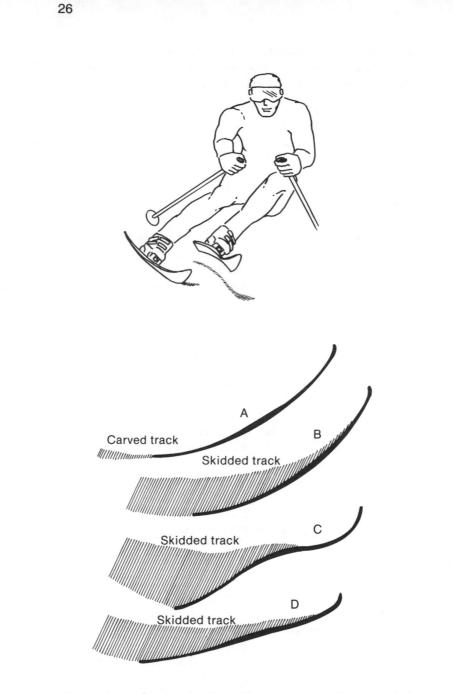

Alpine skis with a soft flex (A and B) can carve easily or can skid. Double-cambered (C) or excessively stiff skis (D) can only skid.

and flex design of the ski. In contrast, *skidding* — sideslipping combined with rotation of the skis — leaves a wide, washed-out track. Therefore, ski tracks tell if a skier carves or skids.

Pure carved turns are not often seen, and only top skiers and racers strive to carve all the time. On the average, all turns will have elements of both carving and skidding.

The skier on page 26 is carving. His outside (right) ski is put on the inside edge by the flexed, pushed-in knee. All the pressure is on the right ski. Notice the camber of the left, unweighted ski and the reverse camber of the right, weighted ski. Carving is possible only on Alpine-type skis (A). Such skis can also skid, naturally (B). Double-cambered skis (C) can only skid. Excessively stiff skis (D) will usually skid, and can carve only with great difficulty.

The prerequisite for carving in soft snow is a ski which can be bent into a smooth-arced reverse camber; on hard snow, a sidecut is an additional requirement. For example, beginners can make carved turns easily in soft snow on short Alpine skis, even at very low speeds. The secret is a very pronounced sidecut and soft flex, which makes the ski easy to bend into a reverse camber.

But what happens if a Nordic ski is stiff or has the *double camber* typical of racing skis (see illustration)? Such skis will inevitably skid *and* be hard to turn, simply because they cannot easily be bent into the proper arc.

Most X-C racing skis can be squeezed base to base with both hands only to a certain degree, leaving a gap in the middle. To make the bottoms touch completely and remove this gap (the double camber) requires a greater force.

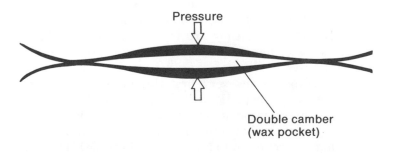

Pressure

Double camber
(wax pocket)

Double camber

Racing skis benefit from this feature since it allows for a contact between the snow and the X-C wax only during the kick, but not during the glide (which would otherwise slow the skis).

From this analysis, it should be clear that the shape of the reverse camber, called *longitudinal flex pattern*, is the most important turning feature in Nordic mountain touring ski design. Unlike Alpine skis, Nordic touring skis don't come with a printed flex pattern, but it is easy to determine. With the tail on the floor and one hand holding up the tip, press the middle of the ski down with your foot. Notice how the reverse camber changes shape with increasing pressure. If it easily flexes into a smooth arc, you can be assured of great fun and easy turning. If it does no more than flatten out, or worse, if it assumes a shape as on the illustrations, you'd better stay on prepared tracks. Stiff or double-cambered skis are difficult to turn and will invariably skid.

You can also check for double camber and stiffness by squeezing a pair of skis in the middle, base to base. While slowly bringing the bases together, sight down the edge of the skis. A good pair of Alpine skis will show full-length contact between the bases, while X-C skis with double camber or stiff middles will not.

Also check for uniform flex, tail stiffness, and in particular tip softness. A very soft tip will be squirrely and unstable when turning. An ideal mountain touring ski tip should be quite a bit stiffer than a typical X-C racing ski's tip. Beware of excessively soft skis. They will be slow on flat terrain and too forgiving on other than easy soft snow. As a point of interest, many good skiers still praise the old wooden skis as the best for turning. No wonder: their flex was great, since no one knew about double camber in those days. But otherwise they are inferior to modern skis— much weaker, heavier, slower, and with troublesome pine-tar bases.

These tests are the very first thing a knowledgeable skier does in a shop. He will discard any ski with the slightest interruption in the smoothness of the reverse camber, since it will prevent carving and smooth turning. Applying this criterion to Nordic skis of course is in direct opposition to the often cited rule, "double camber is necessary for good kick and glide." This concept has no place in

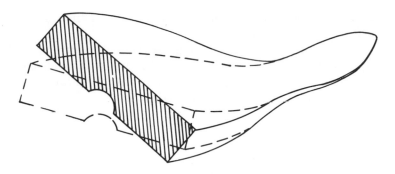

Torsional stiffness of a ski is its resistance to turning at the tip and tail.

backcountry skiing. You need be concerned only about a proper flex for turning on the downhill runs. I have yet to see a backcountry skier, sweating under a 20 kg load, kicking and gliding while breaking trail! He will be shuffling, of course, because it's more efficient.

The Nordic touring skis' *torsional stiffness*, or resistance to turning at the tip and tail, also influences turning. For example, traverse across a gentle, packed slope with the downhill ski weighted and sharply edged. Alpine skis would turn smoothly, leaving a carved path, but most Nordic skis will cut a straight or very long radius path because of their usually low torsional stiffness. The ski does not hold its shape and lies onto the slope, thus nullifying the effect of the sidecut.

A rather high torsional stiffness is desirable to fully benefit from the sidecut. On the other hand, extremely high torsional stiffness can do more harm than good in Nordic skis. The bindings, boots, and ankles, with their own limited torsional stiffness, will collapse under too great a sideways force and cause difficulties in edging, especially on wider skis. More important, excessive stiffness would make the skis more difficult to turn in heavy or irregular snow.

To summarize, sidecut is less critical than longitudinal flex in Nordic touring ski design, but still important. In Alpine skis, it plays a more significant role. The deeper the sidecut, the shorter radius turns can be made. For instance, slalom racing skis have a pronounced sidecut for short turns, while downhill racing skis have a fairly straight sidecut for long turns. Sidecut is the dominant feature on hard snow, while the flex pattern is dominant in soft snow.

Remember, Alpine skis are designed to make turning as efficient as possible. They are meant to turn by themselves, with just a minimum of effort from the skier. If you want to have a ball turning on Nordic skis, look for the Alpine ski-type features.

Choosing the Ski for You

The most widely used rule for choosing Nordic ski length is simple: from the floor to the upraised wrist. But this rule should not be rigidly applied when determining the length of backcountry skis.

For open slopes and Alpine ski areas, the wrist rule is fine. High-speed cruising and long radius turns on packed slopes or virgin powder using 210 or 220 cm long boards is an incomparable joy. Long skis are also best for fast, tele-mark, NASTAR-type races. They are stable, unsurpassed for high-speed carving, and provide the surface area needed in deep snow.

But the wrist rule must sometimes be modified to take into account the skier's weight, ability, and physical condition. Heavier skiers may need a bit longer ski, and beginners and weaker skiers, a shorter ski.

For open terrain and rolling hills, I like to use durable 210 cm racing skis. In a country like Norway, for example, I can "fly" from one mountain hut to another, for days and days. There are food and blankets in the huts, so I carry only a sleeping bag liner, a shovel for an emergency snow cave, and a few other things in a day pack or large belt bag.

For mountain wilderness skiing, including tough terrain, steep slopes, difficult snow, and dense trees, I recommend this rule: your height plus 15-20 cm. That makes 190 cm for me (I am 172 cm). The advantages of such shorter skis are lower overall weight, lower swing weight, and softer longitudinal flex, all making turning much easier and quicker, while decreasing the chance of an injury in a bad fall.

The stability of such skis at high speeds is more than sufficient. Besides, if you plan to ski over 50 km/h in the backcountry, you had better join a Kamikaze club and prepare a last will and testament. There are, unfortunately, more and more reports of skiers with torn-up knees, caused by skiing too fast. The flotation of the shorter skis is slightly less because of the smaller surface. But I think of it as a plus, since I sink deeper into the powder. While the fluff barely touches the knees of skiers on 220s, it flies over my head!

One of the reasons I like shorter Nordic touring skis is that my weight will bend them much more easily, even if the camber isn't quite right. That's how Audun Endestad, a world-class X-C racer, was sold on 190s for deep powder *wedeln* (high-speed, short, parallel turns). When he couldn't figure out why his 215 X-C racing skis were so unturnable, I merely gave him my short pair to try. And his problem was solved.

A much overlooked option is that of compact Nordics. These specialized "brief case" skis are a terrific toy on the feet of an accomplished skier. For mountain terrain,

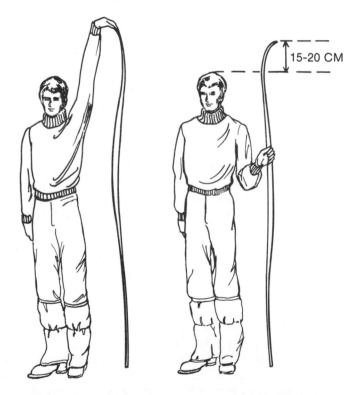

15-20 CM

Use the wrist rule for choosing skis for open terrain. For skiing in mountain wilderness, select skis 15-20 cm above your height.

150 cm is probably the minimum practical length. Stability is, of course, sacrificed, and if you suddenly switch from 220s, these short skis will feel wobbly and sink more when breaking trail in deep snow. But there are some great benefits. They turn almost effortlessly, seemingly with just a wiggle of a big toe. You can go places where nobody else can—deep powder in dense trees, very narrow chutes, "mashed potatoes," breakable crust—since you'll be able to turn very quickly. The chance of an injury is radically decreased, thanks to the lower leverage.

A Nordic compact ski must be designed very similar to an Alpine compact ski, except for a narrower width. Therefore, none of the few existing Nordic compact models are acceptable, only "graduated length method" (GLM) or compact Alpine skis, the lighter, the better. Look for durable junior models; they are narrower. Luckily many ski shops sell or even throw away their old rental models. Plug the holes with steel wool and epoxy, put on Nordic bindings, and *voila*!! You've got a pair of great backcountry skis for next to nothing.

Not surprisingly, my old 150 cm GLMs carve turns very well, thanks among other things to the ice skate effect, the concentrated pressure on the short steel edge, and to the pronounced sidecut. Naturally, they tire my feet more on very hard snow because of their instability. In addition, the extra width requires more leverage for edging.

After having skied on normal length skis, you shouldn't have problems adjusting to compacts. To parallel turn, in particular to telemark wedeln (see Chapter 7), is fun and efficient. Just remember to use the telemark position for stability most of the time.

Not many skiers can afford more than one pair of skis, so the intermediate length seems to be the optimum compromise for use both in Alpine ski areas and in the backcountry. The full-out Nordic mountaineer might consider compacts. My personal preferences are to use 210 cm long skis for cruising and 160 cm compacts for deeper powder in densely growing trees.

Is there an optimum width for Nordic touring skis? Consider the two extremes. For very quick edge changes and increased edge pressure which facilitates quick turns with less effort, a Nordic racing ski's width would be ideal. But then the overhanging boots and bindings would catch in

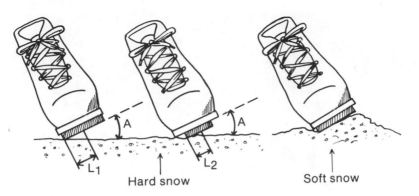

Increased leverage is needed to edge wide skis in all but the softest snow.

the snow, and the flotation might not be sufficient. On the other hand, extra wide skis offer good flotation but put too much stress on the ankles because of the increased leverage needed to edge them in all but the softest snow.

I use an old pair of wide GLM skis for Nordic powder hounding and have great fun, but prefer a narrower ski for firmer snow. The most common dimensions, plus or minus a couple of millimeters, are 65 mm tip, 55 mm waist, 60 mm tail.

All this ski design theory is fine, but it is never a substitute for test skiing. True, if the in-the-shop tests are not favorable, the skis are almost guaranteed not to perform well. On the other hand, if the same tests indicate a good pair of skis, trying them on the snow may produce different results. There are a great number of factors affecting ski design—weight, weight distribution, longitudinal and torsional flex, flex distribution, damping (the ability to reduce vibration), sidecut, and flare angle, to name a few. The final product, the behavior of the skis on the snow, is a complex interrelationship of these factors. There is no ski designer or a computer in the world capable of exactly predicting a ski's "skiability." That's why every new model undergoes extensive testing, both on and off the snow. If you don't want to be unhappy with your equipment purchases, get an expert skier's advice, then try out a few demonstration skis.

I am often asked, "What's the best ski?" This is like being asked, "What's the best pie?" There is none! Some

Author wedelning on Nordic gear in Gore Range, Colorado. (Photo by Naomi Yager)

skis offer a few desirable features, but lack a few others. Some are terrific in powder, but poor on hard snow and vice versa. It is not possible to design a ski perfect for all conditions. Again, the best bet is to try different models, preferably under the conditions in which the skis will most frequently be used. Strive for skis which will be suitable for a wide range of conditions. This generally means soft rather than stiff longitudinal flex, and a rather rigid torsional strength. Such skis will be more forgiving and can be enjoyed in most conditions.

Ski Features

A black base for skis is desirable. It absorbs the sun's energy readily and facilitates applying and removing X-C and Alpine waxes, drying, and adhesion of climbing skins.

A grooveless base makes turning much easier, especially on long skis; applying and removing X-C and Alpine waxes is easier, and a better grip results from the larger area for X-C waxes (or a better adhesion of skins). The stability of such skis at high speeds is slightly less than with grooved skis. You can fill in the grooves (you may prefer to do it only underfoot, for one-third of the length) with P-tex by using a special heat gun—a pretty simple job.

Offset metal edges allow for side filing and are easier to keep sharp. Aluminum, as opposed to steel, edges help to keep the weight to a minimum. Despite the fact that they are softer and impossible to always keep sharp (they are not offset), aluminum edges are sufficient for Nordic touring in all but hard snow conditions. Steel edges are a necessity for more demanding skiing. Skis for Alpine touring, the more full-out sport, always have steel edges. Besides giving an extra bite, metal edges also improve overall durability and strength of the skis.

The feathery weight of Nordic gear makes the search for the freedom of the hills so much easier! No wonder more and more skiers with the heavy and sophisticated Alpine touring gear switch to the "skinnies." Try to keep the weight of all the paraphernalia attached to your feet (the boots, bindings, skis) and to your back at a minimum. The one exception may be on well-groomed Alpine slopes, where extra weight will give you more high-speed stability.

There is an empirical formula about the weight of ski equipment. It says that if you, for instance, put an extra 1 kg on your feet, it corresponds to putting an extra 4 kg on your back. This is merely what basic physics discloses, and skiers everywhere can attest to the validity of the formula after carrying different weights.

After all, the savings on ski gear weight means longer trips (more room for food and fuel) and easier travel.

Waxable or Waxless

I doubt anybody enthusiastic about Nordic mountaineering would consider present waxless models. X-C waxes—or even better, skins—give a much firmer grip on ascents and allow for better glide and turning on descents. Waxless skis are okay for easy trips, Sunday strolls, or occasional racing in 0° C (32° F) conditions, but waxable skis give much higher performance overall.

Bindings

Heavy-duty dependable gear is required to exploit all the techniques needed for the wide variety of conditions encountered in the mountain backcountry.

Bindings must be sturdy and well made. For mountain backcountry, 3-pin Nordic Norm bindings are recommended. Though light 38 mm, 50 mm, or other bindings may suffice in less demanding terrain, the boots which go with them are very light and soft, and the small boot-binding contact area prevents good control.

I prefer bindings with a flat bail, which distributes the pressure evenly over the toe of the boot. It is a good idea to slip two pieces of plastic tubing over the bail to protect the boot seams. To make this task easier, heat the bail, and spray some silicone on it.

Not many skiers bother carrying a posidrive screwdriver, but that's the type of screw supplied with modern bindings. These screws have a cross-head pattern and four points as the Phillips head screws do, but extra metal at each point provides a stronger grip as well as good torque. I always substitute old-fashioned slot-head screws in my Nordic ski gear, since I have a pocketknife which includes an ordinary screwdriver. Since there is a chance of a slot-head screw's being stripped, some skiers prefer the posi-

Bindings for Nordic mountain touring

drive screwdriver, which also holds better. Fortunately, a small, No. 3 Phillips head screwdriver with its tip filed down will fit both Phillips head and posidrive screws. Either way, mount the screws with epoxy glue, but first make sure the epoxy is suitable for the core of your skis by consulting your local ski shop or the manufacturer.

Snow build-up underneath the boot is frequently a problem. To prevent snow accumulation coat the bindings with hot Alpine wax and occasionally silicone-spray them. Stick a ski-width Teflon antifriction plate behind the binding for further protection.

With more people venturing onto steep slopes, there will be more bulletin board notices like this: "One of my skis chose the freedom of the hills. If you find it, please contact Johnny Naive." Who said that Nordic bindings never release?! There is always a chance of its popping loose or losing a bail! Unless you are willing to chase your lost ski, install runaway straps. Unfortunately none of the Nordic bindings have a convenient place to attach such straps. The best way I have found is to drill out the pin in the front of the binding, and in its place attach a strong key ring or solder or weld a wire ring. This provides a convenient place to attach both the runaway strap and a strong short cord connected to the bail. A safety cord on the bail is impera-

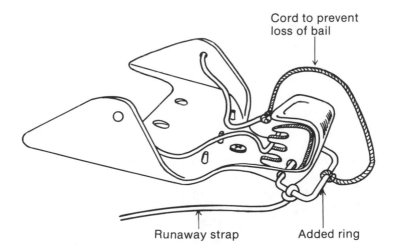

Attaching runaway straps to Nordic bindings

tive, since bails may spring loose and are easily lost. Carry a spare.

Runaway straps like those used for Alpine ski bindings are fine, if operable with mittened hands. So is a strong nylon cord with one or two clips on the end. Fasten the strap around the boot, not to the boot's eyelets or laces, which may pull out. Two holes drilled in the side of the binding will also make it possible to tie or wire the boot to the binding in an emergency.

Nordic binding technology has been at a virtual standstill for the past 20 years. This is to some extent a tribute to the efficiency and simplicity of the classic 3-pin binding. It works, at least well enough when coupled with conventional Nordic boots.

The major complaint has been the lack of a release feature and the generally poor torque transmission of the boot/binding system. Recently, modern technology has entered the scene with a plastic boot-release binding system called the "2-pin," which has the forward flex of a conventional system, but the lateral stability and release capability of an Alpine system. Being suitable for both Nordic and Alpine touring skis, and for telemark and non-telemark turns, the system is the first answer to the need for a rigid, yet light boot/binding system for the backcountry.

Heel Locators

Many skiers know the frustrations of trying to turn and feeling the boot heel slip off an iced-up heel plate and twist like a washrag. There are only two ways to solve this problem: either buy super-stiff (but super-heavy and super-expensive) expedition-type boots; or use heel locators, ingeniously simple devices that represent a true revolution in Nordic gear.

Heel locators are a two-part affair—a spur fastened permanently to the boot heel and a V-notch bracket attached to the ski. Lowering the heel mates spur and V-notch and prevents sideways movement of the boot.

Heel locators have no effect on stride. Turning becomes easier, since the forces are distributed between the toe binding and the heel locator. As an additional benefit, locators save your boot toes and toe plates by eliminating

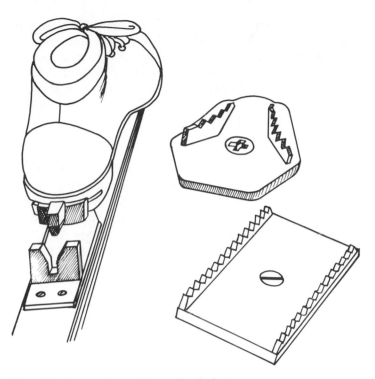

A heel locator and two styles of heel plates

wobbling. In that respect, even very stiff boots benefit from heel locators.

Some skiers call heel locators "cheaters," but this sort of cheating means having full control over the skis, thus minimizing the chance of a twisted ankle.

If you are handy with tools, you can easily design your own locators using aluminum angle. Spurs can be heat-bent from a stiff plastic plate.

Heel locators are very safe, but do increase the torque on your leg as well as on the ski. Other devices which clamp and hold your heels down are extremely dangerous. Remember, what makes up for the lack of release in Nordic bindings is the free heel!

Heel Plates

If for one reason or another you prefer not to use heel locators, then you must rely on heel plates.

Of all the different types, those with serrated aluminum teeth seem to grab boots the best. The biggest problem with these plates is icing over. To combat this, coat the screw heads with epoxy, then hot-wax the entire plate. For a backcountry fix, heat the plates with a candle, and drip hot paraffin onto them. Silicone spray doesn't produce a long enough lasting effect to efficiently curb the problem.

Poles

On undemanding trips you may prefer to use standard Nordic ski poles, preferably made of aluminum; Tonkin (bamboo) or fiberglass poles break too easily. One small modification will make your poles more versatile. Rest each pole on the floor, and grasp it below the grip with your arm bent 90°. This will be the location of a new grip, a

Modify poles for traversing steep terrain.

12 cm wide band of neoprene tape. The new grip, used when traversing steep terrain, "shortens" the uphill pole. The "shorter" poles will also be very much appreciated when turning.

For proper poling techniques, your hands should fit snugly into the straps. Since you will be skiing one day with all the mittens you possess, and another with just thin gloves, it is very important to have easily adjustable nonslip straps.

A note of caution: *Never* wear pole straps on descents, no matter how easy. There have been many accidents where poles caught in deep snow, rocks, brushes, or trees and wrenched or dislocated shoulders. The new breakaway type of strap can release from the pole if snagged and is a great safety feature. Breakaway straps are being added to European ski standard norms, but are not yet required or generally used. I personally am very safety conscious and won't wear pole straps at all during descents, or in avalanche terrain.

Solid baskets with few perforations increase the support in deep snow, and they don't get caught in brush or on your

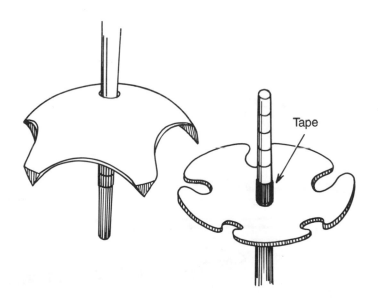

Baskets suitable for Nordic mountain touring

skis and bindings as easily. Therefore, I prefer to use Alpine rather than Nordic-type baskets, even on Nordic poles. To prevent accidental loss, wrap some silver duct tape around the poles just below the baskets. To take the baskets off, just unwrap the tape.

One of the best investments you can make is the purchase of a pair of avalanche probe ski poles. These usually come with Alpine grips; I suggest replacing them with Nordic grips (illustrated below). Both baskets and grips are removable, and the two poles can be joined to make a single, double-length probe. They are a must for serious mountaineering as they can be used for probes if your avalanche transceiver malfunctions (see Chapter 16).

One brand of ski pole designed specifically for ski mountaineering offers four different interchangeable grip styles, a variable length adjustment, and avalanche probe convertability. These poles are most versatile when used with the self-arrest grip (opposite), which works very well on flats, ascents, and descents, while providing the skier with self-arrest capability, a must feature in the backcountry. The length adjustment is an extremely convenient feature. For steep traverses, shorten the uphill

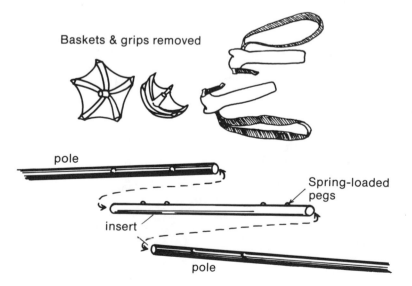

One style of avalanche probe ski poles

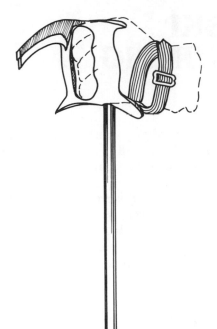

Self-arrest ski pole

pole. For a flat terrain, adjust the poles to armpit length. For turning, shorten the poles so you can hold them with your elbow bent 90°. An ingenious friend of mine found more prosaic uses for this type of pole—as a back scratcher, crutches, a fishing rod, and a flute. Not bad for such a simple piece of gear!

2. SKI TUNING

Taking good care of your skis is as important as keeping your boots dry, clean, and waxed. The rewards will be twofold. The skis will live longer, and they will perform much better.

The new generation of Nordic skis has synthetic bases which require tuning very similar to Alpine ski tuning. Proper tuning will assure that the skis will turn easier, run faster, and hold better on hard snow. This task is quite simple. The basic aims are a flat waxed base, square and sharp edges, and a dulled tip and tail. Here are some useful pointers.

Ensuring a Flat Base

With the ski clamped securely in a vise, move a straight edge over the entire base to see if the base is flat. If the base is higher than the edges, use a scraper to level it. First sharpen the scraper by working it against a file lying on a flat surface, then remove the burrs from the filed scraper with a fine grit whetstone. Now push the scraper in short strokes along the ski to remove the excess base. After every few strokes check for flatness with a straight edge, but do not use the scraper.

If the edges are higher than the base, put a 10 inch mill bastard file across the base with equal pressure on both edges. Holding the file at a 45° angle across the base, draw it from tip to tail. Lift the file from the base after each 30 cm stroke. Continually clean the file with a file card and the ski base with a rag, and regularly check for base flatness with a straight edge.

It is important to draw the file or scraper from the tip toward the ski tail, but start in the tail section to produce an overlapping shingle effect. A whetstone will smooth out the edges and remove burrs.

Some new skis may have rough "hairy" bases which are very slow. The "hair" can be removed and the base made perfectly flat with a rigid wood sanding block covered first with No. 100, then subsequently with No. 150 wet-dry sandpaper. Sand the base smooth with long strokes.

The Edges

Clamp the ski on its side and grasp the file lengthwise and parallel to the edge side. Place your thumb on top of the file with your bent-in fingers on the base to guide the file and assure a 90° edge. File with light pressure, 30 cm strokes, from tip to tail, until the edges are square and sharp. You should be able to shave off a little of your fingernail by scraping it across the edge.

An often neglected but essential step is dulling the tip and tail edges to eliminate overturning and hooking (grabbing) of the skis. Place skis base to base with tails on the floor, and without squeezing them, drop a piece of paper between the tips. Now squeeze the skis so the paper will fall a little, and place a mark 2 cm below the point where it stops. Round both tip edges with the file from this mark forward. Repeat this procedure for the ski tails, and also round the corners of the tail protectors—the metal bars on the ends of some skis. Smooth the entire ski edge with a stone held flat, then clean the base first with a moist and then with a dry rag.

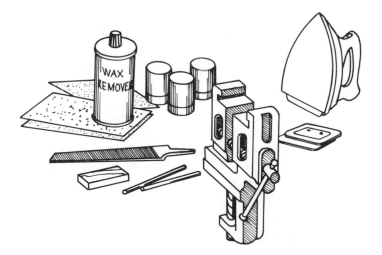

Equipment for ski tuning: scraper, iron, waxes, wax remover, sandpaper, file, sharpening stone, P-tex candles, and ski vise

Base Preparation

If you plan to use only skins and not X-C waxes, melt a soft *glider* (a wax for around 0°C or 32°F) against an iron, and smooth it into the ski base. Set the iron temperature so the wax is on the verge of smoking, and constantly keep the appliance moving to avoid base damage. After the wax has cooled down, scrape the excess off the edges, sidewalls, and groove as well as the base with a sharp plastic (never metal) scraper. This is a one-time-only treatment, to achieve a deep wax impregnation in brand new skis.

Now, apply a hard glider wax in the same way; repeat the application after each trip, or whenever the base starts to look dry. It is important to scrape the excess wax off as well as possible, otherwise the climbing skin adhesive will pick it up. When in the backcountry, apply a thin layer of P-tex liquid wax, which comes in a tube.

If you will be using X-C waxes, rub special green X-C wax onto the entire length of the base, and smooth it in with an iron set on a low setting (permanent press, rayon, synthetic). Let the wax cool down, and scrape it off. To make this layer very thin and smooth, you may additionally use a cork. The special green wax serves as both a glider and a base wax for X-C climbing waxes. (See also Waxing in Chapter 3.)

Regular Maintenance

Check for nicks and burrs caused by rocks and crossed skis. Smooth them out by polishing both sides of the edge with a stone and then filing the edges sharp again, if necessary.

Clean gouges in P-tex bases with a spray wax remover. After the (flammable!) solvent has evaporated, light a P-tex repair candle and point it downward like a pencil, so the flame is blue. Let melted P-tex run into the gouges. When it cools, scrape or file it flush with the surrounding healthy area.

3. UPHILL— WAXES, SKINS, AND WEDGES

On a typical backcountry trip there are often long and steep ascents. But I've noticed many skiers wax as if they were going to race on prepared tracks with double-cambered skis. Later they find themselves herringboning or sidestepping, a most tiring experience.

It's better to forget all about high speed, X-C race waxing in the backcountry. Since the object is to climb long slopes, concentrate on making your skis grip very firmly, no matter how much glide you lose. This means taking an entirely different approach to waxing, or perhaps even using climbing skins instead.

Waxing

As a general rule, choose a wax that is softer (warmer) than the one corresponding to the actual conditions. For example, if the wax chart you're using recommends hard blue, use purple or even red or yellow. In a pinch, any softer wax, including klisters, will work. The secret is to put the softer wax on thinly and smooth it out evenly. It also helps to wax the entire length of the ski, not just underfoot.

The two-wax systems are to many skiers the best choice for the backcountry. The performance of the two waxes is more than adequate, and all conditions can be covered by varying the thickness and roughness of the wax. Since two-wax systems are wide-range waxes, they also resist icing up. To complete the process, add a blue klister for ice or a red klister for wet corn snow. Always keep klister tubes in a plastic bag on a string around your neck to keep them warm. Otherwise, they won't be squeezable.

Besides waxes, you will also need a cork. Divinucell foam works the best. A double-edged scraper is also necessary. One edge should be a stiff stainless steel plate, used for removing waxes. The other edge should be plastic, which is great for smoothing out waxes, especially klister.

To maximize grip, use wet wax, even when dry is called for. And for wet conditions put on a thicker and rougher layer of wet wax. Such maximum-grip waxing is often necessary—as when you're pulling a sled. Skis waxed in this way will get you straight up amazingly steep slopes, often as effectively as skins do; and if you decide to travel in a whiteout, it is often the safest to shuffle rather than glide.

As a general rule, the thicker or the rougher the layer, the better the grip, but so is the chance of icing up. If icing should occur, scrape one ski across the top edge of the other, or try stamping hard on one ski while gliding it forward, preferably on an icy patch. Anyway, iced-up skis make ascending very easy.

Once on top of the slope, scrape the wax with a sharp metal scraper, but be careful not to damage the base. If you ski with a friend, you can do this (as well as waxing) for each other, without taking off skis. Removing the wax with a good scraper is easy. Further cleaning of the skis with a liquid wax remover or white gas is superfluous. The remaining thin wax layer won't prevent good glide and will even give sufficient grip for climbing back up an already-packed trail. Of course, if you are a downhill speed demon, you might want to run a glider wax over the entire base.

While waxes are synonymous with Nordic skis, there is no reason why they cannot be used with Alpine touring skis. However, the P-tex base on Alpine skis is different, and waxes do not adhere to it as well as to Nordic skis. To reduce wax wear, first roughen the entire P-tex base with 150 grit sandpaper. Alternately, you can use a special X-C wax binder or apply X-C waxes with the heat of an iron, stove, or candle.

Climbing Skins

Climbing skins are generally considered to be an integral part of Alpine touring, but a Nordic mountaineer may be much better off with skins than with X-C waxes when on long steep slopes and particularly on extended trips, where energy savings may be considerable. However, rolling hills require putting the skins on and taking them off repeatedly. In this event, X-C waxes are a better choice.

Climbing skins are like the hair on a dog's back. Run your hand one way and the hair lies down and your hand

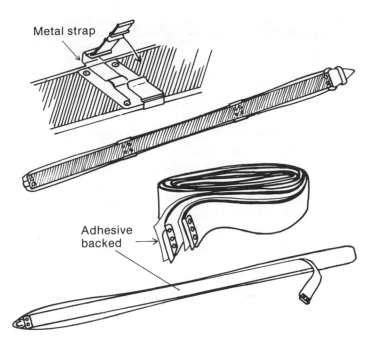

Metal strap

Adhesive
backed

Climbing skins: strap-on (top) and glue-on (bottom)

glides across. But run your hand the other way and it catches on the hair.

The first climbing skins were made of deer hide; later, seal skin was popular. Luckily for seals, the fur of a modern climbing skin is made of wool mohair or of polypropylene laminated to a sturdy backing. The trend has been toward increased performance and considerably lower weight.

There are two main types of attachment: the strap-on and the much more popular glue-on. Glue-on skins are held in place with a tacky adhesive. They are simpler and lighter than strap-ons, and snow will not build up between the ski and the skin. But the adhesive has to be protected from wax and other contamination.

Here are a few pointers for using glue-on skins. They will hold only on bare bases or well-scraped Alpine waxes. X-C wax must be removed from the skis before the skins are applied, otherwise the adhesive on the skins will become contaminated and lose its properties. Keep the skins clean. Dry them with the hair toward the sun, since ultra-violet rays damage the adhesive.

A climber made from rope, an alternate to skins

It is a good idea to attach a set of Velcro tail straps to each skin. Such straps make it possible to use the skin even if the adhesive is old and doesn't stick. Attach a piece of black stick-on Velcro ("hooks") to the skin tail (which wraps up over the ski tail). Fasten the Velcro part ("loops") to the ski top, under the skin tail.

A roll of 2.5 cm white cloth-backed adhesive tape is the best skin repair material. It can be used to repair or reinforce worn areas and can be wrapped around the skin and ski if the adhesive fails. I strongly recommend carrying along as a backup a small amount of universal or wet (from the dry-wet system) X-C wax and a small amount of skin adhesive. The wax can become very handy if the skins get lost or damaged.

If you are a budget-conscious Nordic skier, here's a trick. Wide Alpine skins may be cut in half for your Nordic skis, halving the price as well. But skins narrower than half the width of the skis don't grip well.

An inexpensive or emergency climber can be made with polypropylene rope. First attach the tail part. Then, bend the ski into reverse camber and attach the front loop so the front part of the climber is on the binding side; push it over to the other side. Keep the rope climber tight by adding a knot or two. The more knots, the more traction.

Wedges and Plugs

To take full advantage of the skin's capacity, some Alpine bindings offer climbing plugs, spacers which fit between the boot heel and the ski. They make steep ascents as easy as walking upstairs. The relaxed, level foot position allows climbing extremely steep slopes with less ankle strain and with remarkably less effort.

Since Nordic boots are not very rigid, a simple heel plug lifter wouldn't be adequate. However, I have designed a similar heel support device for Nordic touring, a wedge which fits between the binding and the heel locator and is

A homemade wedge for steep ascents

strapped onto the ski. It can be made of a light high-density foam or a similar material.

Paul Ramer, the designer of Ramer Alpine touring bindings, is presently designing a variation of my wedge idea. His is made of aluminum plates, is adjustable, and incorporates teeth for extra grip on very hard snow. It resembles the *harscheisen* (crampons) used with Alpine touring bindings.

With both climbing skins and wedges, tackling steep slopes becomes quite easy. No more herringboning, side-stepping, or strained feet!

4. ONWARD AND UPWARD

There is more to backcountry skiing than just ascending and descending. Quite often flat or almost flat terrain separates the skier from his destination.

There is an old saying, "If you walk, you can Nordic ski." If it were absolutely true, so many skiers wouldn't be making so many mistakes on the easiest trails. Even many telemark kings can't properly do a simple diagonal stride. When people put on skis, they amazingly tend to do the most unnatural things. While you may not be concerned with achieving X-C world champion style, you should strive for correct natural techniques that result in easy, efficient, energy-saving skiing with a pack.

Let's compare correct techniques with the most common energy-inefficient mistakes. Remember, recognizing mistakes is an excellent method of learning. If nobody is around to tell you what to improve, then evaluate your own

Shuffling

technique by observing your reflection in a window of a house or watching your shadow in the early morning or late afternoon.

Shuffling and the Diagonal Stride

In the backcountry, you will be shuffling rather than kicking and gliding 99.9 percent of the time. In unbroken snow with a heavy pack or sled and a full day of skiing ahead, trying to imitate a racer is self-destructive; shuffling is the only way. It is as natural as walking—relaxed, upright, arms swinging back and forth, but not in an exaggerated manner.

Want to go faster? Just lean forward more and try to jog, first with very short, quick strides, later with longer ones. Get the feeling of pressure underneath the ball of your rear foot. Master this first technique without poles, later with them, and make sure the movements feel natural and relaxed. Concentrate on forward lean and arm extension, long strides, and a powerful kick, pressing down and back with the rear foot. This is the diagonal stride.

The natural simplicity of the diagonal stride is obvious. Unfortunately, the majority of skiers try their best to make it harder and more complicated than it is, think-

Diagonal stride

Mistakes in the diagonal stride

ing they look like racers. Above, for example, many errors are apparent.

This skier's front arm is reaching too far forward, while his rear arm isn't extending far enough behind; both extensions should be similar. His stride is too long. His rear leg is stiff and straight, while his front foot is too far forward. The front knee should lead, or there will be no weight shift from one foot to another, as there is in walking and jogging. His back is too straight and stiff, and there is no forward lean.

The skier's right hand is gripping the pole too tightly and too low. He should shorten the pole strap, lightly squeeze the pole between his thumb and index finger just below the knob, pushing with the strap. Alpine skiers in particular don't know this technique, since they use poles for turning only. The skier's left hand is also gripping the pole too tightly and in an incorrect fashion. He should put his hand through the strap loop from below and check that the strap is not twisted.

The skier below is making some other common mistakes. His skis are too close, forcing him to use his poles as outriggers, when they should be used mostly for pushing. The correct ski spacing is about 15 cm, as in racing tracks, and the skier's hands should almost be touching his legs. He is obviously swinging from side to side and bouncing up and down. Try to keep the upper body still.

The most efficient way of getting rid of these bad habits is to do a lot of jogging on skis on a slight uphill. Forget you have skis on, and think only about jogging, using short quick strides, first without and then later with poles.

Balancing mistakes

Double poling

Never use a diagonal stride on descents or on fast snow on flats. You will go faster and with less effort if you double pole or skate.

Double Poling

Double poling is used quite often for crossing icy lakes and skiing gently slanted tracks in the backcountry. When performed correctly, it is a very simple maneuver (see skier above).

Swing your arms forward, bend at the waist, and let your upper body fall onto the poles. Now extend your arms behind you, and push on the straps with only a very light grip on the poles.

This skier (top, page 57) is demonstrating the most common mistakes. He has squatted into a sitting position instead of simply bending forward. His head is lifted, straining his neck. He is gripping his poles tightly instead of pushing with the straps. When the technique is performed correctly, the poles will not fly up, as his have, but will be extended straight back.

The Kick Turn

There are at least as many ways to do a kick turn as there are skiers, but you should learn the correct, safe method.

Stand across the slope, so that your skis don't slide down

Double poling mistakes

the hill either forward or backward. Face downhill and plant both poles as shown below, *without* changing your normal hand grip. Lean on the straps of the poles, lift the downhill ski, and turn it around. After placing it on the snow, lift the uphill ski and turn it around *without* moving either pole. Now you may do whatever you wish with the poles, but only after achieving a stable position. If the slope is steep, it may be helpful to first stamp out

The kick turn

two flat steps below you for a more secure finish to the turn.

The usual causes for falling during a kick turn are not leaning on the pole straps enough, keeping knees and legs too stiff, and moving the poles too soon.

On steep terrain you may prefer to execute uphill kick turns, especially when using skins. These are performed facing uphill instead of down.

The Pretzel Turn

If you have ever eaten pretzels, the looped and twisted kind, you'll understand where this turn got its name.

With your body facing uphill, move your downhill ski across the uphill and cross your legs. Then lift your uphill ski and reposition it. Sounds acrobatic, doesn't it? But it is good for stretching and is fun.

Uphill Skiing

There is nothing sophisticated about skiing up a slope. Wax the skis for maximum grip or put on skins, use the shuffling technique, and you'll be on the top of that beautiful powder bowl in no time.

The pretzel turn

Avoid sidestepping or herringboning up a slope because these are the most tiring ways to get up. If your group uses widely different ski gear, let the skiers with skins go first and put in a track, one which is not too steep for anyone to follow.

I would like to stress that the group always should follow the experienced leader in a single track only. There are two reasons for this: aesthetics and avalanche safety, which will be discussed later. Many strangely shaped tracks zig-zagging up a mountain make the mountain ugly. They are literally scars in an environment that should be left un-touched and visually unspoiled. Isn't it more appealing to ski down a slope of untouched snow, rather than trying to cut figure eights in a bowl chopped up by uphill tracks?

Just Plain Walking

In the spring or summer, the times of corn snow, it is often easier to hike up a slope and haul the skis behind. But skis and poles, when not used for skiing, can be a great nuisance. One solution is to slide them through the special slots provided on many packs, or to strap them onto the pack. Alternately, you could tightly tie the skis bottom-to-

60

bottom with a strap around the bindings and carry them in one hand with the poles in the other. You can also slide one pole through a binding, loop its strap over the ski, and carry a pole/ski unit in each hand.

Many experienced backcountry skiers drill a hole in the tip of each ski, which enables them to haul the skis behind them when walking on hard snow. Such holes make it easier to convert the skis into an emergency sled. Drilling the holes won't affect the skis' performance in any way, as long as the insides of the holes are coated with epoxy to protect the inner core of the skis.

(Right) Author demonstrates aggressive up unweighting in heavy snow

5. THE TURN— UNWEIGHTING METHODS

Unweighting means removing body weight from the skis in oi ₋er to turn them more easily and quickly. It occurs in the majority of parallel and telemark turns. There are several methods of unweighting, and I will describe here some of the most popular techniques. They should be studied carefully, since unweighting is one of the most important parts of skiing. Without it, turning is very difficult and often impossible.

Up Unweighting

Up unweighting is most common of all methods and the easiest, especially for beginner-to-intermediate-level skiers. It is accomplished by a simple quick extension of the body, just like in an upward jump. At the highest point in this hop, the unweighting is at its maximum, permitting easy turn initiation.

Most powder skiers unnecessarily exaggerate this technique by bobbing up and down with arms flying

Up unweighting on Nordic skis

everywhere. Though unnecessary in light powder, such excessive and aggressive unweighting is vital in heavy snow, where the skis have to be lifted completely off the snow surface between turns to allow edge change and easy turn initiation.

Nordic skis usually require stronger unweighting than Alpine skis. For example, while parallel turning to the left in heavy spring snow (opposite), I aggressively up unweight, completely freeing my skis from the snow. As I finish my left turn, I drop into the telemark position for stability.

Telemark turns also make use of up unweighting. The skier rises after finishing one telemark to initiate another, then gradually sinks again after changing directions.

Leg Retraction Unweighting

This is the fastest unweighting technique, a sudden pulling up of the knees using abdominal and back muscles. Peter Bambini from Perisher Valley Ski School, Australia, demonstrates leg retraction with an easy exercise (below). Starting with a relaxed position, just as though finishing a right turn, he retracts his legs, thereby causing unweighting. After his skis have reached the highest point, he twists his legs to the left for a smooth transition to another turn. Practice this exercise as Peter does and it will be

Leg retraction exercise

easier to apply on the snow. Think of your legs as pistons, pumping up and down and twisting.

Here's leg retraction in action (opposite). The lifting of the skis from the snow by the upper body is enhanced by the rebound push of the skis as they spring back from the reverse camber flex into their normal relaxed shape. This added lift is much like the action of a springboard.

Down Unweighting

When explaining down unweighting to ski school students, one instructor likes to ask the question: "Can you recall promenading on a beach barefoot and suddenly stepping on a stone?" What happens? You instinctively drop to unweight the foot, right? That's down unweighting.

You have undoubtedly used the same technique skiing over moguls, absorbing ("swallowing") them by suddenly lowering your seat and flexing your knees. Down unweighting is also useful on smooth terrain to initiate turns.

Terrain Unweighting

Bumps, moguls, and uneven terrain provide other unweighting possibilities. When your feet are on the top of a bump, they can be easily twisted since the ski tips and tails are off the snow. You can further increase this unweighting effect by using bumps to become airborne.

(Left) Leg retraction in action

6. THE TURN — BASIC TECHNIQUES

For practicing turns, choose a soft-packed, smooth, and gentle slope with minimum ski traffic. Some of the lower runs at Alpine ski areas are ideal. Rather than sitting in a chair lift and freezing, walk up the slope to keep warm and stretch your muscles. When you master the basics, switch to ski lifts for faster progress. But be prepared for snide remarks in the lift line: "Excuse me, what happened to the other halves of your skis?" "Pardon me, your heels just came off your bindings . . . ."

The basic stance in all turns is of greatest significance. An excellent way to learn it is in front of a mirror, without skis on. Try to assume a relaxed and flexible, never locked or stiff, position.

You might be surprised how a 15-minute stretching session will improve your performance. Such stretching of leg, back, foot, and shoulder muscles before and after skiing, is especially valuable on backcountry trips, where muscles often stiffen up from the cold and from vigorous activity.

A final word: you won't find here step-by-step instructions for elementary techniques. Describing basic wedge and stem turns could well make another large project. If you are an absolute beginner, please refer to one of the many excellent instructional books on Alpine skiing. Even better, attend a ski school; but don't be afraid to take Nordic, rather than Alpine skis.

The Telemark Turn

The telemark, the easiest turn to learn, will assure you enjoyable skiing in most conditions. From my experience in instructing, I have found that a skier of average talent who knows basic X-C flat track techniques can be taught rough, linked "tellies" in merely 15 minutes! It is that easy. In contrast, parallel turns require much more time to learn.

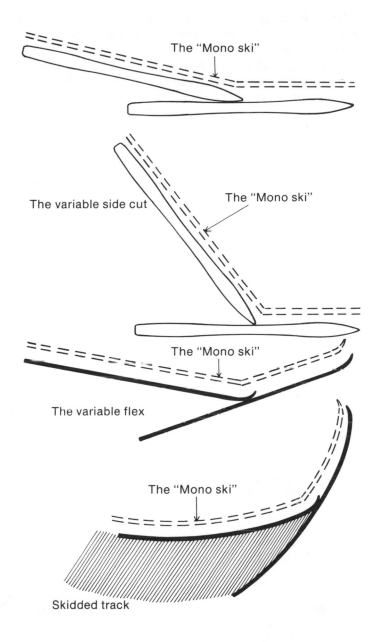

The "Mono ski"

The variable side cut

The "Mono ski"

The "Mono ski"

The variable flex

The "Mono ski"

Skidded track

The telemarking "mono ski"

Before jumping into a description of technique, an understanding of how the telemark turn works, theory so to speak, is an asset.

You can look at a pair of telemarking skis as a "mono ski," (page 67) an imaginary ski bent in the middle around the point where the back ski touches the front ski. As you change the angle between the skis, in effect you are varying the sidecut and longitudinal flex of the mono ski. This interesting feature is found only in the telemark turn.

As discussed in the Nordic Ski Design section of Chapter 1, these two features, sidecut and longitudinal flex, are the main factors in turning. The more the sidecut, the sharper the turn; the softer the longitudinal flex, the easier the turn.

Notice also another important phenomenon: the greater the angle between the skis, the more uneven the curve of the mono ski becomes.

When the skis are almost parallel, long radius carved turns are possible. Increasing the angle between the skis

Telemark practice

results in a sharper turn, but skidding caused by the "break" in the mono ski is unavoidable.

The first step in learning the telemark turn is practicing the telemark position. Traverse a slope using a wide parallel stance. Slide one ski forward, and drop the trailing knee down until it almost touches the rear ski (opposite). The forward knee should stay ahead of the forward foot. Make sure both skis are equally weighted. Bounce up and down to get used to the flexible telemark position; it will feel uncomfortable, unnatural, and tiring at first. Now raise up and reverse the skis, so your other leg leads.

It's helpful to recognize the most common mistakes. Below the skier's forward foot is ahead of his knee and his front knee is not bent. His trailing leg is straight and stiff, and his arms are flailing.

Mistakes in the telemark position

Telemark turn

Once you begin to feel comfortable and fluid performing this exercise, you can move on to the telemark turn.

Choose a flat area on which to practice. Assume the correct telemark position, and move the forward ski ahead of the tip of the rear ski and at a slight angle to it. This angle is most essential, since it causes the skis to turn. Maintain this telemark turn position, and start double poling. You will be turning!

Notice the important inward bend (drive) of the front knee (opposite).

Learning by double poling has several advantages. You'll be traveling at a very low, safe speed and learning correct arm and pole position, which helps balance. Do these turn exercises to both sides. After mastering them, try linking left and right turns, first on flat and then on gentle slopes.

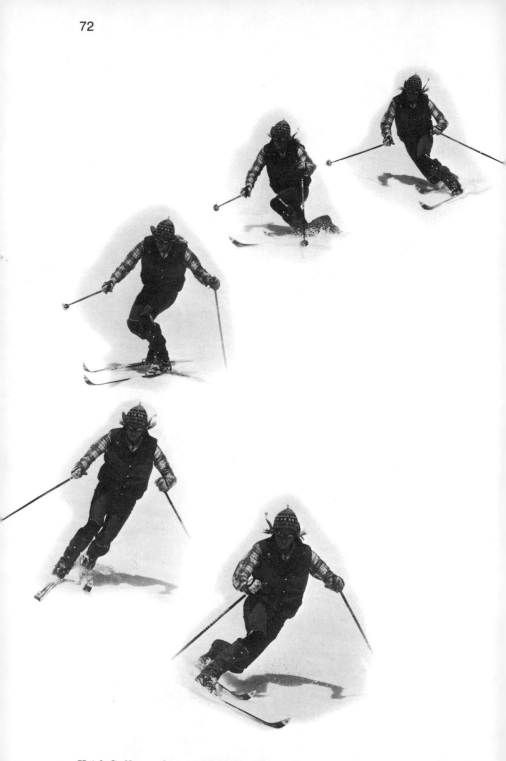

Keith Calhoun demonstrates the telemark turn.

After a few days of practice you will be turning like this king of the mountain, Keith Calhoun (opposite). Keith is in the middle of a right turn. His left knee is bent drastically forward and inward, steering the ski. His right knee almost touches the right ski. As he finishes the turn, he plants the left pole to initiate a new turn and up unweights with the aid of the rebounding skis. While unweighted, he changes the leading ski by striding the right foot forward. This is the most tricky part of any telemark. He then sinks down, pressing his right knee inward and forward to turn. His skis are held parallel most of the time, which allows them to carve.

Study the second frame from the top carefully, and retain it as a positive image in your mind. Keith is demonstrating an excellent stance, essential to efficient, enjoyable, high-performance telemarking. His upper body is erect and relaxed, facing downhill at all times. His arms are relaxed and in full control, not flailing wildly. His hands are held low and well forward so he can see them. His skis are weighted equally and edged.

If you are having problems learning to telemark, they most likely are the result of an incorrect telemark turn position. Keeping your skis too parallel may inhibit turning at lower speeds. The more wedge between the skis, the sharper the turn. Overturning can be the result of several errors—holding the telemark turn position too long, too great an angle between the skis, or not enough weight on the back ski.

The Parallel Turn

With the forgiving short skis of today, many beginning Alpine skiers learn rough parallel turns in a few days without knowing anything about snowplow or, as they are currently called, wedge turns, and stem turns. But wedge and stem turns should not be regarded as for the beginner only. On the contrary, every skier should master them and use the different turns required by ever-changing conditions. Eventually, however, you will want to add the parallel turn to your repertoire.

The most important aspect of learning the parallel (or any) turn is correct body position (below). Ankles and knees should be flexed, weight evenly distributed between the balls and heels of the feet, and the skis apart. Check your technique in a mirror at home.

Opposite is the basic parallel turn with a down-stem. After finishing the previous turn in a relaxed stable stance, the skier flexes his legs and pushes out (down-stems) the outside ski. Simultaneously, he moves the downhill pole forward, mainly by cocking his wrist. After planting the pole, he extends his body, which unweights the skis and makes them easy to pivot. He continues to turn by gently pushing his knees and ankles in the direction of the turn. Soon the skis are again parallel.

The vast majority of mountain skiers do not think parallel turns suitable for Nordic skis, but I heartily recommend learning parallel turns on the skinny boards. Hardcore telemarkers may be persuaded to try parallel turns if they understand that their legs do not have to stay together like

Correct body position for the parallel turn

the Alpine skiers'. The history of modern skiing attests that for many years, good skiers of all kinds kept their legs comfortably apart!

To Telemark or to Parallel

I don't feel it right to rank the parallel turn above the telemark turn or vice versa. It is much better to learn both techniques, know how they work and realize their advantages and disadvantages. Remember that the more

Basic parallel turn with a down-stem

techniques you know, the more versatile skier you will be, which means safer, more enjoyable skiing. Comparing the main features of the two techniques illustrates the uses, problems, and positive aspects of each.

COMPARISON OF TURNING TECHNIQUES

Telemark Turn	Parallel Turn
ORIGIN	
Unique to Nordic skiing	Very similar to parallel turn on Alpine skis
LEARNING	
Very easy to learn	Takes time and effort to learn (easier for Alpine skiers)
STANCE	
The skier's stance is not a natural, athletic one; stronger legs are needed; the turn is more tiring; the back knee is sometimes injured by hidden rocks or stumps.	The stance is natural, athletic, "ready for action."
STABILITY (FORE-AFT)	
Excellent	Poor. To improve stability, one can assume telemark position.
STABILITY (LATERAL)	
Gets poorer as the skis become parallel. Usually not a problem when a skier goes very fast.	Very good
WHEN TO USE	
Best suited for cruising, long radius turns; quick turns are much more difficult.	Very short (wedeln) as well as long radius turns are almost equal in ease of performance.
EFFECTING THE TURN	
The radius is effected mainly by changing the angle between the skis and by twisting (the feet and the knees).	The radius is effected mainly by edging and twisting, and by the ski design.

Telemark Turn	Parallel Turn

DIFFICULTY OF TURNING

More difficult in narrow chutes, on very hard snow, in dense trees.	More difficult at very low speeds or in cruddy snow.

TYPE OF SKIS

Turns can be made on any pair of skis.	It is more difficult to turn if the skis don't have Alpine characteristics (sidecut, longitudinal flex, etc.).

CARVING TURNS

The technique, by its nature, is not quite suited for carving because the two skis face two different directions! One of the skis (and quite often both, as on page 67) will skid. What contributes more to skidding is that the adjustable sidecut and flex are quite uneven, i.e., not an arc; the skis can't be edged as much as in a parallel turn; and it is impossible to weight only one ski. At the most, a skillful telemarker may be able to carve one ski at a time. The only exceptions—and when the telemark feels really good—are long radius, high speed cruising turns with skis parallel (or almost so). That's carving!	**Alpine skis:** The turn is well suited for carving if the skis have Alpine turning characteristics. When a weighted ski is edged, its side forms the shape of an arc on the slope. The less a skier is able to follow that arced line, the less he carves and the more he skids. **Nordic skis:** Since the present Nordic skis generally have little side camber and are stiff, one should ski fast and only on the outside ski for better carving. The skier's entire weight and centrifugal force will bend the ski into reverse camber and assure better edge hold.

EDGING

Edging by pressing knees inward is limited. Further edging can be accomplished by banking (leaning entire body inward) or hip angulation (leaning hips inward).	Edging can be done by banking or hip angulation, but knee angulation (pressing the knees inward) is by far the most efficient edging technique in modern skiing. It allows for very sharp edging and quick turns.

Stepping and Skating Turns

A technique which is being overused by Nordic skiers is the snowplow, or wedge turn. In my opinion, the wedge and wedge turn are dangerous and too tiring in anything other than soft-packed snow. They often result in head-first splashes, broken skis, twisted ankles, and other disasters. Use them only as a last resort. Even walking down a narrow trail may be easier! Replace them with the stepping and skating turns described below.

Stepping and skating turns, though simple, are quite often neglected or never properly learned by most skiers. Perhaps they seem too elementary to bother with; nevertheless, they should belong in the repertoire of all skiers.

For an easy direction change while gliding, or to come to an uphill stop when gliding down a gentle slope with snow too difficult to turn in, just make short quick steps to one side. That's the stepping turn.

Skating and skating turns are accomplished in the same manner with skis as on ice or roller skates. They differ from stepping turns in that the skier must more actively push himself off the inside edge of the ski. For extra speed, double pole while skating; it's an efficient way to move on flat or gentle slopes with a heavy pack.

Carving

Carving is the trademark of an accomplished skier, yet it doesn't involve anything that an average skier cannot do. I stress carving throughout the book because it should be the ultimate goal for all skiers. True, it may be unnecessary on the groomed slopes of Alpine ski areas. But in the backcountry, where the only grooming is made by skiers' sitzmarks, the ever-changing conditions necessitate correct techniques, like carving.

It is great fun for Nordic skiers to ride ski lifts—and there is nothing wrong with it, because they can learn the turning techniques more quickly and safely on commercial ski runs than in the outback. But there is some danger of overdoing it. Groomed slopes invite sloppy techniques that won't work at all when ski touring.

I strongly recommend that Nordic skiers try Alpine ski gear to get the feel of carving. But I also suggest that they ski outside the packed runs in difficult conditions such as breakable crust, heavy, or "mashed potatoes" snow.

Considering the design of present-day Nordic gear, carving is easier on Alpine and Alpine-touring equipment. Because of their torsional softness and/or lack of sidecut, many Nordic skis won't carve at all on hard snow. In deep snow they may, since longitudinal flex will play a more important role than the torsional stiffness and sidecut. (See the Nordic Ski Design section in Chapter 1.)

Assuming you have a suitable ski, here's how to make it carve. While parallel skiing on a hard-packed slope, gently roll the outside ski onto its inside edge, put your weight on it, and wait. Presto—you are carving! By utilizing the ski's design, its sidecut and ability to be bent into reverse camber, you can let it turn for you, without much effort. As Horst Abraham, a noted ski theoretician, puts it, "It is like swaying from side to side to turn a bicycle, instead of a hurried turning of the handlebars."

Try this technique on gentle slopes with hard-packed snow. An excellent exercise is to try carving while riding uphill on a surface lift like a T-bar, Poma, or rope tow. Look at your tracks and see for yourself if you are a carver or a skidder. Also, find out if your skis are able to carve at all.

If this approach to carving doesn't work, you may be making some mistakes. Perhaps you did not flex your outside knee forward and inward enough; try to ride only on the ski edge. Or perhaps you put too much weight on the inside ski; try to use it, unweighted, only for balance in the wide stance. Did you push the ski out or twist it, rather than letting it turn by itself?

The arc of a pure carved turn equals the arc of the bent ski, which most of the time is longer than is practical for recreational skiing situations, especially in the backcountry. But the average turn is not 100 percent carved. Typically, it consists of a skidded initiation, the change of direction, and a carved completion. Realistically, most

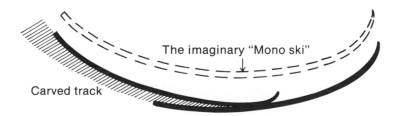

Alpine-type design allows carved telemarks

carved turns have an element of skidding throughout, although it is possible to make graceful pure carved turns without any skidding at all. But they must be fast and of a long radius.

One of the ways to make pure carved turns in heavy snow is this. As you finish one turn on the completely weighted outside ski, step onto the other, soon to become the outside, ski. (This step, called lateral projection, is also described in Chapter 8 of this book.) Then initiate the next turn merely by changing the edge caused by rolling the knee in. The initiation can be facilitated by down un-weighting. Put all your weight on the outside ski to bend it into a sharp reverse camber.

7. THE TURN — ADVANCED TECHNIQUES

After mastering the basic telemark and parallel turns, there is no reason to stop improving. The better skier you become, the wider your ski horizons will be, far beyond what you probably thought. This is what makes skiing so exciting and ever challenging. Although I have skied for many years, I still look forward to learning something new.

My friends often ask me, "Don't you ever get bored with skiing?" I spend two winters each calendar year, one in the Northern Hemisphere, one in the Southern Hemisphere, and rarely see much summer. But I love a wide range of winter sports—Nordic and Alpine touring, mountaineering, X-C racing, Alpine racing, and skiing out-of-bounds. Undoubtedly, if I were to stick to only one kind of skiing, I would be bored to death by April.

Here are some techniques for the better-than-beginners to the expert. All are used by the avant-garde of modern ski mountaineering. Some I developed myself, while others I learned during my many years of skiing all over the globe. Many of the new turns for the "skinnies" combine the advantages of the parallel turn, the telemark turn, and the telemark position. Some of the techniques described can be used with Alpine as well as Nordic touring skis, while a few, the telemark-related turns, are impossible to perform on Alpine touring skis, unless you ski with your heels free which is rather rare.

I would like to emphasize the great value of Nordic skis as the tools for learning almost any technique. No matter which turn you are working on, you will be forced to do it correctly, or you will fall. An Alpine skier supported by his error-tolerant, rigid gear can afford rough, incorrect techniques in all but very difficult conditions. Nordic skiers have no choice but to rely on the finesse of their skills. With this philosophy I have organized a special "first

Nordic—then Alpine" ski school which has experienced great success.

When working on technique, try skiing in somebody else's carved tracks or between trees, or making figure eights. Racing gates are also helpful and will prepare you for the natural gates of tight trees.

The Reverse Telemark

As already noted, parallel turns on Nordic skis lack fore-and-aft stability. The remedy to this problem is very simple—turn with the uphill ski slightly forward. In other words, do an otherwise normal parallel turn, but in the telemark position. Besides this use of the telemark position, the reverse telemark has no other relationship to a telemark turn.

As I ski across a mogul field with a heavy pack (opposite), my compact Nordic skis are less stable than long skis, so I improve their stability by assuming the telemark position. The uphill ski is ahead. I then absorb a mogul by down unweighting and start another turn. While turning, I push the other ski forward into another telemark position.

Observe these few very important basics. My upper body is quiet, always facing downhill in anticipation of the next turn. This body position is sometimes called a gorilla stance—aggressive, ready-for-action, compact, like a coiled spring. My lower body does most of the job when turning. My knees and feet are well bent and angulated, pressed inward for easy twisting and good edging.

Nearly all of ski instruction could be condensed into "Bend ze neez!" Nothing is more important than a good basic stance with well-bent knees and ankles. I prefer to ski parallel rather than telemark, and my friends, seeing me reverse telemark most of the time, started calling it the Polish telemark. (I was born in Poland.)

The reverse telemark

The Telemark Wedeln

This is an ordinary wedeln executed in a telemark position, which tremendously helps longitudinal stability. By definition, wedeln are very tight and quick parallel turns. Therefore, there is no time to change the leading ski to telemark position; wedeln with the same ski always forward to avoid the critical lead change phase of the telemark turn. How much forward depends on conditions. In heavy snow, deep powder, or uneven terrain the telemark wedeln approaches the appearance of a telemark turn, with the rear knee close to the ski.

As I finish a short turn to my left (opposite), my skis are comfortably apart; the left ski is forward and the right heel lifted. I plant the pole and start turning to the right, accomplished mainly by twisting my feet and knees. When learning, exaggerated up unweighting movements, bobbing up and down, make this technique easier. Notice that even as I finish the right turn and am ready to plant my pole and start the left turn, my left ski stays constantly forward. The turns are very fast and short, with only about a second between the first and last turn in the illustration.

When turning to my right, I look as if I am telemarking, but the mechanics of the turn are parallel-like. When turning to my left the technique is identical to the reverse telemark.

Which leg to keep forward is up to the individual skier. It is a good idea to master this technique both ways, so that either leg can be forward. Everyone is stronger on one side of the body than the other. The tendency then is to use that side most often and neglect the other weaker side.

The telemark wedeln is the only proper technique for skiing deep powder in densely growing trees. It allows the quickest possible turns and excellent stability. I should not have to add that it is my favorite turn.

(Right) Telemark wedeln

The para-mark

The Para-mark

The para-mark is another interesting technique, combining parallel and telemark turns.

Here I am in the middle of a left turn with the uphill ski forward (above), which makes it a reverse telemark. As I finish the left turn, I plant the pole and prepare for a right turn. Without changing the lead ski, I start turning to my right, telemark fashion. At the end of the turn, I am ready for another left reverse telemark, with the left ski always leading.

The para-mark, which first may resemble the telemark wedeln, is a medium-to-long radius turn coupling a parallel turn with a telemark turn. The telemark wedeln, on the other hand, is a pair of very quick, short radius, parallel turns performed in telemark position.

When I first introduced the para-mark in America, my friends called it a lazy technique and quite rightly so; it doesn't require a lead change, the most difficult part of telemark turns.

The Deep Powder Wedeln

"Deep powder"—the nicest morning sounds. Once you have tasted the delicious silky feeling and the exhilaration of floating through deep powder, you will always search for it.

Most accomplished skiers agree that deep powder is one of the easiest conditions to ski. This may sound paradoxical, if you have tried the fluff and spent the day crashing every five meters. The secret is that *only correct carving techniques and proper equipment will do*! Skidding and other bad habits may be okay on packed slopes, but not in deep powder.

One of the most enjoyable methods of skiing powder is the true wedeln, an Alpine skiing technique easily adapted to Nordics. The true wedeln involves simply a rapid tight succession of parallel turns.

Here are a few basic and important points (opposite). My upper body remains quiet, facing down the hill, and compact, like a coiled spring. My skis are equally weighted, close to each other but never squeezed together. Notice how my legs wiggle (wedeln) beneath my trunk. My knees and ankles, well bent, accomplish the turn by twisting.

I unweight by leg retraction, a most efficient technique for deep powder. Up unweighting, which is easier to learn, and down unweighting can also be used.

The deep powder wedeln on Nordic skis is the same as on Alpine skis. Only when the snow or terrain gets uneven will you have to resort to the telemark wedeln, as I do at the end of the sequence where I encounter a slight bump and have to instantly assume a telemark position in order not to be thrown forward.

(Right) The deep powder wedeln

The Step or Jump Telemark

On steep slopes, breakable crust, or heavy snow, there may be no choice but to literally jump from one telemark to another.

After completing a left telemark, Keith Calhoun (below) is in the middle of his first jump/step over, with his right ski following and turning in the air.

A telemark with strong edge set follows, as Keith plants his left pole, ready for the next jump.

The step or jump telemark

The step or jump telemark on the steep

Above, Keith demonstrates this technique, called a step or jump telemark once more on a steeper slope.

Notice these essential points, common to both sequences. Keith's upper body and hips always face downhill. His arms are low and to the front, in full control; many skiers look as if they were chasing butterflies. A very good way to develop correct arm and body position is to set both poles rather than one when initiating a turn. Finally, he edges and weights his skis equally when completing the turn.

The Windshield Wiper Turn

The windshield wiper turn is borrowed from Alpine skiers, who most often use it in heavy or breakable snow and in steep narrow gullies, called corridors by French

The windshield wiper turn

mountaineers. Learning the windshield wiper turn is quite easy, if you know parallel turns. Practice on a gentle slope, but imagine you are on a very steep one and there is not much room to turn. Set the edges hard by pressing your flexed knees inward, and jump aggressively. Try to come to almost a full stop after each quick and short turn. In other than soft snow, most skiers keep weight on the outside, downhill ski; but some extreme skiers prefer to *start* a turn by weighting the uphill ski more.

On Nordic skis, I keep my uphill ski forward most of the time to improve longitudinal stability. Such a slight telemark position makes this technique similar to the reverse telemark turn. Since the snow is deep, slushy, and heavy (below), I have to use pronounced up unweighting by extending and jumping around; to increase the effect of the up unweighting, I retract my legs by pulling my knees up.

As I turn, notice the pronounced hip and knee angulation for sharp edging of the outside ski.

So Nordic skiers, go for it! The conditions, admittedly, cannot be as radical as for Alpine tourers, but you will still be able to ski some extreme and mind-boggling slopes.

For Impossible Snow

The technique for crud, ice, or unskiable rotten snow is to "Bend ze neez and get the hell out of it!"

This ingenious and easy-to-learn method (no photo sequences necessary) was developed by my friend Keith Calhoun, one of the fastest telemarkers in the U.S. It always works, says Keith, no matter what. So, if you find yourself on top of such an unskiable slope, go elsewhere. Walk down or glissade (see Chapter 9), or just wait for the spring melt, unless you are a potential suicide victim.

Seriously, I have never been in a situation where I couldn't find easier-than-impossible skiing conditions. There is an infinite variety of slopes and snow types in the mountains; there is no reason to look for trouble and ski in dangerous snow.

8. "LET'S BOOGIE"

Don't be surprised when you discover that this section seemingly doesn't have anything to do with backcountry skiing. If you give it some thought, you will conclude that anything which improves your skill will be of benefit in the backcountry.

I describe here techniques that may very well be the rudimentary basics of a Nordic freestyle. As "skinny skiing" continues to grow at an amazing rate, so do the number and size of Nordic festivals, which include orienteering, telemark racing, costume contests, freestyle, mogul mashing, and the like.

Many of the "tricks" I describe belong to the repertoire of an Alpine ballet skier, while some are unique to Nordic skiing. Practicing and doing them is great fun. More important, they develop better balance and safe recovery techniques. They teach you how to turn on one ski, either the outside or the inside, and thus make you a much better all-round skier.

I cover only the techniques that have value and meaning to backcountry skiing. So you won't find "helicopters," inverted backward flips, and jumps.

Telemark Races

These races are conducted on standard NASTAR courses, originally designed for Alpine skiers. But only Nordic skis with pin bindings, and telemark turns, are allowed. If a gatekeeper catches you not in a telemark position when passing a gate, it costs you a time penalty.

Obviously, these races don't have much in common with the wilderness, but the advanced techniques are useful in backcountry skiing, and the races themselves are becoming quite popular. They also demonstrate the high level of proficiency attainable by telemarking skiers. Some telemarkers even manage to win silver or gold NASTAR medals when competing with Alpine skiers.

Top-notch telemark racers prefer heavy, laterally stiff boots and long, heavy, laterally rigid skis. They often wear shin and knee pads for protection.

A frequent problem in telemark racing or any high-speed telemarking is a frustrating chattering of the skis. This excessive vibration of the skis may result in loss of control and skidding. If not always totally preventable, chatter can be dramatically decreased by starting the turn with most of the weight on the front ski and finishing it while transferring more weight to the back ski, but this technique takes time to learn. It also helps to edge the back ski as much as the front, though many people seem to forget about the significance of the back ski. Starting the turn gently and continuing it in a smooth, unhurried way, letting the skis turn by themselves, will also reduce chatter.

Advancing from the basic telemark to telemark racing requires lots of downhill mileage. Keep skiing and working on your basic techniques. There are no secrets, really.

Lateral Projection

Ski racers often use a technique called lateral projection, demonstrated (opposite) by Art Burrows of Frisco, Colorado. After completing his right turn and passing the gate, he aggressively pushes (projects himself) forward and to the right. This projection provides a higher, better line for the next gate and permits him to unweight and accelerate, even on a gentle slope. After completing the step, he moves into another telemark turn.

Lateral projection

Keith Calhoun demonstrates lateral projection.

Keith Calhoun uses lateral projection even more dramatically (opposite) to set his line for the next, rapidly approaching gate. (A few extra ski poles are used as the training gates.)

Lateral projection is not as difficult as it may sound. It is simply a skating-like motion used when changing from one telemark turn to another. Less advanced skiers would merely change the leading ski by sliding it forward. Lateral projection allows you to ski faster and to choose a different place to start your turn. Of course, it is not reserved for telemarks only; it can be used with parallel turns for avoiding obstacles in the backcountry and simply for getting rid of the common habit of skiing rigidly instead of dynamically.

Turning on One Ski

There may be situations, luckily rare, when you will be forced to ski on one ski, for example, a broken or lost ski, or an injury to one leg. If you have not tried turning on one ski before, you may find it quite tricky.

Practice by keeping one of your skis off the snow all the time while attempting to make a few turns on the other. It should not be too difficult provided you can parallel turn, but learn to turn both directions on either ski. Use the poles for balance and up unweight more than usual for easier turn initiation. Learning to turn on one ski is a prerequisite for many of the maneuvers to follow.

The Cross-Over Telemark

Have you ever accidentally crossed your skis when tele-marking, and felt your rear ski's tip slide behind the heel of your lead boot? The remedy: don't fight it; just start turning in this crossed-over position.

The first step in learning the cross-over telemark is practicing simple cross-overs. Ski down a very gentle, almost flat slope; lift one ski (say, the right); and cross it over the left. Then lift the left ski and cross it over the right. Repeat this exercise many times, until you feel comfortable doing cross-overs.

The next step is to combine a cross-over with a turn. After crossing the right ski over the left, assume a tele-mark turn position. The right ski will be leading, with more than half of your weight on it and with some angle between the skis. The larger the angle, the sharper the turn. Keep turning to the right until you slow down to a comfortable speed; then do another cross-over to regain your normal leg position.

The cross-over telemark

The Outrigger

This technique may be useful when recovering from a fall. Traverse a slope with your downhill leg extended in an outrigger position. Pull that outrigger in under your seat and turn on it, while extending the other leg into an outrigger position. It is important to have all of your weight on the inside (turning) ski, as evident in the illustration (below) by the shadow under my outside ski.

The outrigger.

The royal christy

The Royal Christy

In ordinary parallel turns, the weight is either on the outside ski or on both skis. For a change, try to make parallel turns with most of the weight on the "wrong," inside ski.

As you progress, try the turn with the outside ski completely unweighted and free of the snow. When you've lifted it as much as you can, that's a royal christy!

This superb balancing exercise will enable you to recover from very tricky situations in difficult snow. It also teaches independent leg action—using one leg at a time for turning. Alpine racers sometimes resort to turning on the inside ski, which they call *cramponage*.

The Charleston

The royal christy is a medium-to-long radius turn. A very similar but short radius turn is called the Charleston. Since the turns are much quicker and shorter, there isn't enough time to lift the outside ski all the way. If you watch a skier boogie in this way, the resemblance to dancing the Charleston will be striking!

I recommend first learning the royal christy, then gradually decreasing the radius of the turns until they become short and fast.

(Right) The Charleston

Tip Drag Wedeln

This maneuver is quite similar to the turning-on-one-ski technique described previously, but may be easier because of the support from the dragging tip.

Begin with a cross-over, then lift the trailing ski and let its tip drag in the snow behind you. Get used to this weird position by skiing down a gentle slope with the tip cutting a groove in the snow. Then attempt to make long radius turns. Decrease the radius of the turns until you wedeln.

Did you say you couldn't see any backcountry use for this technique? Imagine this scene, which is not uncommon. A skier suddenly realizes his skis are spreading apart in a big V. If he panics, his crotch will be in danger. But he doesn't. Instead he quickly lets one of his skis go back, dragging its tip on the snow. The recovery is easy, and he makes an uphill turn to stop.

(Left) The trip drag wedeln

9. FALLING!

It is important to know how to fall, how not to fall, and how to stop yourself when you fall.

Some falls are less painful than others. On Nordic skis, falling forward, flat on your face, is the worst kind of a spill. It can be very dangerous and should be avoided at any price by assuming a telemark position.

The sitz fall

The Sitz Fall

The safest way to fall for you, the skis, and the poles is uphill, with your bottom pointed sideways and backward, absorbing the impact. Keep your arms high and forward. Trying to support yourself on your poles and arms invites the chance of breaking them. No straps, remember? And keep your skis well away from beneath your body.

Recovering

Many of the freestyle techniques described in the previous chapter can pull you out of a potential, if not actual, fall. Below, for example, the hours spent practicing the outrigger position will pay off.

Recovering from a fall

The vertical plane turn. (Photos by Gnurps)

After a fall in deep powder, it is easy to get hopelessly stuck; but this predicament also can be easily avoided. If you feel that falling forward down the slope is inevitable, don't fight it. Relax, and let the gravity and the momentum roll you over in a somersault; then get back on your feet. Sometimes I relax too much and the momentum takes me through two roll-overs! It's so much fun that I occasionally do it on purpose.

I call this technique the vertical plane turn, and when I first tried it, I almost choked to death. No, not because of the fluff, but from laughing. To prevent the fluff from sneaking in underneath your parka, install a "powder crotch drawstring"—a short piece of elastic connecting the front and the back bottom edges of your parka.

The ski glissade

The Ski Glissade

Even the most wacky skiers will stop and think twice before attempting a slope that seems to be too dangerous for turning. Such a slope doesn't necessarily have to be an almost vertical wall. The combination of blue ice, 20° chute, and cliffs or crevasses below, for example, can be much more threatening than a 50° open slope filled with soft corn snow. Another dangerous condition is depth hoar, a breakable crust that barely supports two skis but gives up under the weight of one.

The technique for such situations is the ski glissade, basically sideslipping with one pole acting as a brake and outrigger. Place the poles together, basket to grip, and hold them with one hand close to the braking basket, the other a bit higher.

Dig the point of one pole into the slope, and lean on it. By distributing the weight evenly over the two skis and the pole tip, you should be able to sideslip on very bad breakable crust.

The ski glissade position may be quickly changed to self-arrest (page 114) whenever a need arises.

The self-arrest

The Self-Arrest

Ever steeper and ever more difficult is the trend among extreme skiers. They ski places that make ordinary city dwellers faint—steep walls, seemingly 90° couloirs, and other forbidden reaches—often shocking climbers ascending the same slopes with crampons, ice axes, and ropes.

But a released binding, equipment breakdown, loss of concentration, or hidden rock may cause a sudden loss of control. In steep terrain, stopping the ensuing fall may make all the difference between life and death, especially if there are cliffs, rocks, or crevasses below.

When you lose control and feel that rolling over is inevitable, don't fight—utilize your momentum and roll over *instantly*. If you hesitate any you will quickly reach the speed of a rocket.

If you are using ordinary ski poles, drop one pole and grab the other with both hands close to the basket for maximum leverage. Gradually dig in the pole point; keep the pole close to your body so you can lean on it with your full weight. All the while, keep your ski edges free of the snow. Do not attempt to use them for braking until you are nearly stopped. Otherwise they may catch and send you into an uncontrolled tumble.

The self-arrest is much easier with special self-arrest poles. These poles have a protruding spur molded into the hand grip, which serves the same purpose as the pick on a climber's ice axe (see page 43). After a fall, swing your skis below you as quickly as possible, then force the spurs into the snow. But do it gradually, or the poles may be jerked from your hands. And again, don't brake with your ski edges or a flip might ensue. To be effective, the braking spur should be at chest level and no higher, with your full weight driving it into the snow.

Self-arrest ski poles in use

II.

alpine
ski
touring

10. ALPINE TOURING EQUIPMENT

When you've reached your limits on Nordic gear and wish to move on to steeper, more difficult terrain, Alpine touring may be the answer. With Alpine gear, it is possible to handle much greater difficulties. Let's begin with an equipment review.

Boots

There are several approaches to boot selection, and all have their proponents among Alpine tourers.

Many tourers use their climbing boots for skiing; however, they are not the safest for use with release bindings. Climbing boots are usually not rigid or high enough to transmit the dangerous forces to the binding and effect a release. This may result in injuries, even if the bindings are performing properly. With nonplate bindings, the release is further affected by boot-to-binding friction. Even with the safest bindings, using climbing boots is like coupling a 200 W hi-fi amplifier with 5 W car speakers.

There are, however, obvious advantages to wearing climbing boots in the high mountains, and the hazards can be reduced by using short skis (less torque) and the lowest practical release setting. It may be even safer to use free-heel cable bindings or simply not to clamp the heels down; this provides a vertical quasi-release as in Nordic skiing. But free-heel turning will require more finesse.

The rigidity of a climbing boot can be increased by using plastic shells which clamp on over the boot. Called "spoilers," these shells make skiing easier and transmit forces to the binding more efficiently.

At the other extreme is the conventional Alpine ski boot, as used on lift-serviced slopes. These plastic boots offer the highest degree of stiffness, can be very light, and can be bought inexpensively. I don't recommend them for long climbs since they are very uncomfortable, but they are great for shorter trips.

A few people still use the old-fashioned, all-leather, double Alpine boots, which went out of fashion when plastic technology took over. Depending on their age, they may be as effective as ordinary climbing boots or the more modern plastic boots. Testing these older models on the snow may be the only accurate method of assessing their effectiveness.

There are also boots specifically designed for Alpine touring. Generally they consist of a plastic shell, a leather

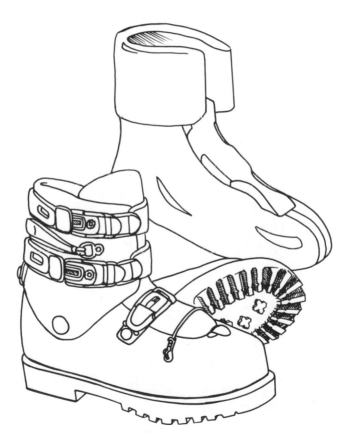

Double boot designed for Alpine touring

or foam/felt innerboot, hard-rubber lug soles, and a buckle adjustment for either comfortable walking and climbing or for downhill running. Innerboots made of closed-cell foam are extremely light and warm and are the ultimate choice for high-altitude mountaineering. Wool felt innerboots are sufficient for most conditions and have the unique ability to keep feet warm even when wet. If you find such boots too warm, remove the innerboots and insert neoprene foam insoles and washable wool felt insoles.

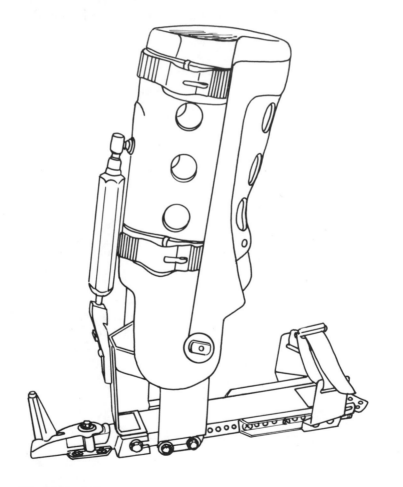

The MotiveAider

In a class of its own stands the unique boot/binding system called the MotiveAider. The binding has a cuff-type extension which will fit over any footwear from climbing boots to rubber shoes. It is intended for the most demanding skiing.

Incidentally, a black boot or liner is better than white, since it will warm up more easily in the morning sun.

Bindings

Long gone are the days when cable bindings reigned supreme both on the lifts and in the backcountry. They were rightly called "legbreakers" because of their unreliable release. Nevertheless, they can still be seen on many touring skis. They are simple, lighter than most, accommodate any boot, bend forward up to about 90° when ascending, and are inexpensive.

The newer models of Alpine touring bindings show the designers' concerns not only for minimum weight, but for maximum safety and reliability. Compared to the "legbreakers," they provide a much more reliable release, but their design lags behind modern Alpine bindings, especially in their release capabilities. A well-known ski binding engineer summarizes the situation: "Present Alpine touring bindings face the same problems as Alpine bindings of a decade or so ago; their usually fixed ratio of different releases is a disadvantage."

The features to look for in an Alpine touring binding are multi-angle release for both ascent and descent (generally, the more release angles the better), sufficient vertical and lateral elasticity to prevent inadvertent prerelease in rough conditions, an adjustable climbing plug or lift for steep ascents, ease of operation when switching from ascent to descent, sturdy simple construction, and light weight. Ideally, the binding should be approved by either TÜV, IAS, or BfU, European norm-setting bureaus for skiing safety.

There are two categories of modern Alpine touring bindings: the plate and the nonplate.

In the plate binding, a plate is firmly attached to the boot. When a release occurs, the plate (with the boot) comes out of the binding. Release is affected only by the binding's mechanism and not by the boot's shape, stiffness, materials, or boot-to-binding friction. Therefore, this binding provides the most uniform release.

With the nonplate binding, the boot itself is released just like with step-in Alpine bindings. The release can be affected, and in extreme cases even prevented, by the way the boot's shape and other characteristics interact with the binding.

When mounting bindings, use glue to seal out moisture and to stop any vibration between the ski and screws. Use anaerobic glues which cure in the absence of air, such as VC-3, Vibratite, Lock-tite, neoprene glue, or yellow waterproof carpenter's glue. Epoxy glues are necessary for honeycomb-core skis and they provide a bomb-proof mounting. But exercise caution whenever using epoxies since they will damage some foam-core skis.

Use antifriction devices like Teflon pads with nonplate bindings whenever possible to reduce friction and to make the bindings safer.

Each day, check for loose screws and missing or bent parts. Lubricate with a silicone or the lubricant recom-

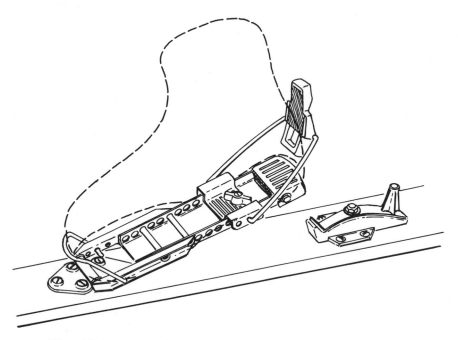

Plate Alpine touring binding

mended by the manufacturer. Before skiing, do a release check. Can you twist your foot out of the binding? Can you pop it by quickly bending your leg forward, standing on only one foot with no one standing on the ski? With nonplate bindings, make sure the boots are clean and seated properly so there is the least possible friction between them and the bindings.

It's a good idea to carry some assorted tools, spare parts, quick epoxy with steel wool, and bailing wire. They can be a real lifesaver. Even in the most dramatic breakdown, some wire will often keep the equipment together.

Skis

As ski mountaineering grows in North America, so does the choice of skis. Now many manufacturers offer specialized skis for Alpine touring. Their design stresses the lowest possible weight combined with easy handling both in powder and in difficult snow and terrain.

But many Alpine tourers simply use compact recreational Alpine skis. There is actually almost no difference

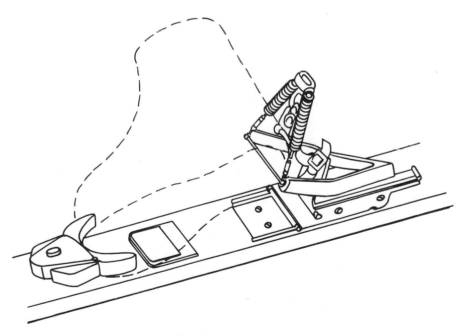

Nonplate Alpine touring binding

between them and the specialized Alpine touring skis. These short skis are easy to turn, and some lightweight models are excellent choices for backcountry skiing. A typical honeycomb ski, for example, weighs only 2.1 kg per 160 cm pair, less than most steel-edged Nordic touring skis.

"Baby-sized" skis are quite popular among European climbers. They bear the name *Firngleitern*, which means "corn snow gliders," and are intended for summer glacier skiing. Their normal length is 130 cm. Personally, I find them too wobbly; the minimum practical length for me is 160 cm.

There are many good reasons to use shorter skis for the backcountry: lower overall weight, lower swing weight, less leg-breaking torque in a bad fall, easier handling. True, the trade-off is some loss of stability at higher speeds, but a compromise is unavoidable. Remember that when you are way out in the mountains, you should be skiing much more slowly. Also keep in mind that a perfectly safe binding has yet to be invented.

In Europe, the birthplace of ski mountaineering, most people prefer shorter backcountry skis. A few famous

Harscheisen *plate*

skiers, like Sylvain Saudan, still use long boards (210 cm), but they are exceptionally strong physically and superb skiers. Tim Tucker, one of the photo-sequence demonstrators in this book, had a chance to ski with Saudan and enjoyed it immensely. But Tim was able to ski some narrow, 45° corridors while Saudan was unable to follow simply because his 210s wouldn't squeeze in.

The best way of finding the optimum length ski for you is by experimenting. You may even come to the conclusion that long skis are worth the extra sweat and other disadvantages.

Accessories

Most of the accessories discussed in Part I, Nordic Mountain Touring, fit in nicely with Alpine gear. The steeper terrain, however, may require such items as self-arrest ski poles, climbing skins instead of waxes, and heel lift plugs.

Alpine tourers often add *harscheisen* to their equipment list. These small plates bent into a U-shape fit over the ski under the boot or binding. The serrated edges of the plate protrude beyond the base of the ski into the snow and provide extra grip on icy slopes.

11. EXTREME SKIING

Extreme skiing, an activity halfway between skiing and mountain climbing, is to some the most glamorous aspect of ski touring. What are the special thrills of skiing the super-steep? The immense concentration, the beautiful mountains, and the pushing of body and mind to the upper limits to meet a challenge all make the extreme skier look for more and more difficult ski descents. You have to experience this fantastic feeling to realize that extreme skiing is something special, and not only because few people do it. An extreme skier must be a master of the mountains, know more about avalanches than average, and be an expert at skiing.

"Skiing the impossible" is a much more popular activity in Europe than in America, mainly because backcountry skiing has always been more popular there. European skiers like Patrick Vallencant and Sylvain Saudan, who have skied Mt. Everest, Mt. McKinley, and other exotic places with slopes in excess of 63°, have received a great deal of publicity through the press and movies. There are superb extreme skiers in America too, but they tend to be little known.

Most people prefer Alpine touring setups for extreme skiing. Doing it on "skinnies" is feasible, but much more dangerous because the overhang of Nordic bindings can grab in the snow and throw the skier out of balance. I have skied slopes of around 53° on Nordic gear, but the conditions were always perfect, with no observable danger. Most of the time, Alpine gear is the only reasonable choice.

Since the releases of present Alpine touring bindings are often unreliable, some skiers prefer to use ordinary Alpine bindings and simply walk up the slope, often with crampons and ice axes. Whatever bindings are used, they should be adjusted to the maximum practical release setting to prevent pre-release, and runaway straps should be securely fastened. If a plate binding is used, the heel clamp

Sunset on the Fox Glacier, New Zealand

should be strapped to the boot to prevent accidental release from heavy or crusted snow. Loss of a ski is one of the most frustrating and disastrous events that can befall a couloir skier. For this reason, many skiers lock their bindings so there can be no release at all. The trade-off, of course, is the possibility of injury should a release be needed.

The skis must be well tuned, with the edges sharp and smooth and the bottoms waxed for good glide, which will make for easier turning and safer skiing.

The dangers encountered in extreme skiing are avalanches and the consequences of a fall. Needless to say, ski only when there is no avalanche danger. The best snow is in the spring or summer, when the top layer of a thoroughly hard-frozen snow cover has been warmed for an hour or so by the morning sun, creating a 2-4 cm surface layer of soft corn snow.

Avoid snow that acts like it might slough. Sloughs are small loose-snow avalanches that involve only the top layer of snow. Often harmless, sloughs can become very dangerous if they knock you down and take you on a leg-breaking ride over cliffs or into crevasses. They may also trigger a dangerous deep slab avalanche.

If the snow appears to be saturated with water and is not cohesive ("rotten snow"), it can slough anytime and can easily turn into a wet avalanche, a real killer. Another dangerous situation occurs in spring and early summer. The snowpack seems to be strong, but the layer just above the ground is not, and free water percolating there may release a huge ground avalanche. The best way to prevent an accident is to check the soundness of the slope by digging a snow pit.

Because of the much higher avalanche danger in the winter, steep chutes are skied mostly in the late spring and summer months, when the most dangerous conditions are breakable crust, hard névé (consolidated granular snow changing slowly into glacial ice) with a thin wet top surface, and of course, ice.

Some areas offer better snow for extreme skiing than others, like the coastal ranges of America, Australia, New Zealand or Norway. There the snow is often packed firmly by the wind and can be very strong because of the high humidity and the relatively high temperatures. This is not to say, though, that monster-sized avalanches don't occur in those places!

After making sure that there is no avalanche danger, prepare exact plans of the route up and down. Study the area on the map and also in the field. The ideal slope has an outrun which is perfectly safe, so in the case of a hopeless fall, you would only tumble down and stop on the flat surface, without encountering cliffs, crevasses, rocks, or trees. By way of some magic, even a single tree on the slope will surely come after you should you fall.

The Ascent

The prerequisites for extreme uphill skiing are climbing skins in good repair and Alpine touring bindings with tall climbing plugs. Not all snow conditions will permit extreme ascents. Fresh powder, wet corn snow, and powdery

windpack are not good for steep climbing. The best climbing snow—wet spring snow, and dry summer névé—
makes climbing angles of up to 50° possible. Yet while
possible, such steep ascents are not practical. See for yourself what the most efficient and comfortable angle of
ascent is.

Some bindings are equipped with unusually tall climbing plugs that provide a heel-to-ski angle of about 28°, so
that a 40° slope feels no steeper than a 12° incline. The net
result is the illusion of climbing a flight of stairs. Typical
climbing rates at this angle are between 300 and 500
vertical meters per hour, with minimal fatigue and muscle
strain. This compares very favorably with other forms of
ascending snow slopes. However, it is still preferable sometimes to climb on foot with the aid of crampons and ice
axes.

At the start of a steep pitch, make sure your climbing
skins are securely attached. There is nothing more disastrous than having a skin peel off near the top of a steep
climb. The tail straps and hardware of nonadhesive skins
must be in excellent condition, since they must withstand
most of the shear forces. If adhesive skins are used and they
are too short to wrap around the tail of the ski, wind some
adhesive tape around the skin and ski. This can also be
done with nonadhesive skins if the ski does not have a
notch for the tail strap. Do not wax or silicone the skin's
mohair as is often done to improve glide, since this will
prevent the skis from climbing as well.

When climbing, distribute your weight evenly. Shifting
your weight forward or to a ski edge is an invitation for the
skin to slip. With your weight forward, recovery from a slip
is very difficult. Take short rather than long steps to improve weight distribution and save energy.

It is advisable to break your own trail. It's easier to get
traction if the snow has not been packed, though one of the
few exceptions is fresh powder. In any case, check the
traction on and off the beaten trail. Never follow directly
below another skier because he might slip.

Gently slapping the ski into the snow with each step is a
useful technique, but slapping too hard can cause loss of
grip. Smooth weight transfer from one ski to the other
reduces the chance of slipping. If a serious slip does occur, it

can usually be halted by a quick step down and across the slope.

The best route for extreme uphill skiing is usually straight up the fall line, the line of steepest descent. If the snow is soft, a herringbone or a forward diagonal sidestep can sometimes be used to negotiate obstacles. If the snow is hard, route finding is very important; any deviation from the fall line will cause a slip. Careful use of ruts, suncups (depressions melted by the sun), sastrugi (wavelike formations in the snow), and other discontinuities in the slope can make climbing much easier. Attempt to keep most of the ski flat and in contact with the snow. Therefore, if a course change is required on very steep snow, it's best to sidestep or traverse. Dirty snow will frequently provide better traction than clean snow.

Only on relatively soft snow is it possible to ascend steep slopes diagonally. To maintain better balance on such a traverse, set the uphill binding in the regular touring position and the downhill binding in the climbing position. This height difference gives the effect of a level track, but can generate tremendous torque on the bindings if a slip occurs.

During steep climbing the ski poles are used primarily for balance and recovery from slips. Variable length poles should be shortened or a second, lower hand grip should be installed on standard poles, since it is difficult to use a long pole on a steep slope. On very difficult pitches, the spurs on self-arrest grip poles can be firmly planted in the snow and used as an assist, much as in ice climbing. Unless great care is taken, leaning on the poles will reduce traction and actually precipitate a fall.

The Descent

Most skiable chutes and headwalls vary in steepness from 45° to 55°, though short pitches often exceed 60°. The difficulty and danger involved, however, are more a function of snow conditions, obstacles, and exposure than of steepness alone.

Only one skier should be in the chute at any time. The others should maintain vantage points where they can observe the skier in case of a slide or fall. In long chutes, the first skier can sometimes stop and wait partway down, if there is protection from sloughs, rockfall, and falling skiers.

If the condition of the snow is questionable, or if there is no route into the chute without going over a cornice, the first skier in should be roped and belayed. He can then proceed to ski check the first 10 meters or so, kicking off any unstable snow. Determine the conditions beforehand by poking through the snow with ski poles, by noticing the color and texture of the cover, and by observing changes in weather, steepness, and slope orientation that may affect the snow.

Each skier has to plan where and how sharply to turn. Once in the chute, any technique that will get you to the bottom in one piece is the right technique; you should have had lots of practice on short safe pitches before trying any extreme descent.

High speeds are dangerous. You should complete each turn and be almost stopped before starting the next turn. This will allow dislodged snow to go on past you after each turn instead of building up behind and creating forces that might cause a fall.

If the snow is sloughing badly, the start of every turn may create a slough that will block the completion of that turn. In this case, it is best to give it up and sideslip or glissade to the bottom. If you discover too late that an avalanche is threatening, ski close to the edge of the slope, not in the middle. Never try to outrun an avalanche!

When you notice an icy patch, don't try to turn on it. Slide over it, then turn on the softer snow beyond. Occasionally it may be better to plant both poles, rather than one, to start a turn. Learn not to lean onto the poles; try to merely touch the snow with them. A few skiers have been killed because their poles became stuck in heavy snow or a snow crack and threw them out of balance.

Falls can and do occur, and they are difficult to stop on a steep descent. Once off your edges, you will accelerate as fast as a sky diver and in a few seconds be falling so fast that only natural obstacles will stop you, usually with significant personal damage. Self-arrests are not always possible. Wet, sticky, early spring snow is difficult to ski on and causes more frequent falls; however, if the snow is in this condition, a fallen skier will not slide but will simply stick where he falls.

Protection against and recovery from falls are of utmost importance on firm snow. Many spring and summer chute skiers wear crash helmets and loose high-friction clothing. Nonskid clothing will slow acceleration during a fall and provide a few moments more to regain footage. Short pants and shirts are only an invitation to lose a lot of skin.

Packs should be close fitting and secured tightly with a waist strap. When skiing rough terrain a loose pack can easily cause loss of balance. Theoretically, a quick-release waist strap will allow the skier to dump his pack if necessary; in practice there just is not enough time for such maneuvers.

The chute skier must have very fast reflexes. On a 50° slope it isn't possible to fall in the recommended uphill position, since the skier is in too close a contact with the snow with his uphill hand and arm. Most frequently he gets his weight too far forward or back, or catches a downhill edge on an obstruction or rut, any of which will throw him into a head down position. The only hope of recovery is a self-arrest. A high-friction jacket and gloves are of immense value in this situation.

The best recovery device is the self-arrest pole. Some skiers fasten a small ice axe to a pole shaft or even ski with an ice axe in hand, a practice which is cumbersome at best. The self-arrest pole hooks do not interfere with skiing at all and are instantly ready for fall recovery without requiring any change in hand position.

Extreme skiing is but one part of the incredibly broad spectrum of mountain experiences available to the responsible mountaineer. But if you are not an expert skier, don't even try this challenging activity, and never rely on self-arrest to get you out of trouble. Extreme skiing is safe only for masters of a no-falls technique.

Remember, though, extreme skiing is not necessarily any more desirable than the gentlest tour or downhill run. People ski the backcountry for a dozen different reasons. That's the beauty of the sport.

III.

the
mountain
environment

12. PERSONAL EQUIPMENT

It is easy to get so involved in ski equipment and ski technique that you lose track of an important point. The mountains are an unfamiliar and hostile environment posing many dangers to the ill-informed and the ill-prepared. In the mountains, your survival depends on what you take with you, and it's possible to take too much as well as too little.

A check list for equipment and food may not seem to be very important, that is until the day someone fails to bring a stove or fuel or a tent or whatever and everyone in the party is left in an uncomfortable, perhaps even dangerous situation. You can prevent such occurrences very easily by referring to a personal and group equipment list. Don't trust your memory even if you have camped thousands of times before! "Sicher ist sicher," as Austrian mountaineers say, which can be loosely translated as "Play it safe."

A check list appears in Appendix A for your convenience. Since this book is not meant to be a primer for basic winter wilderness skills (some of the many fine books on the subject are referenced in Appendix B), I'll talk here only about some selected pieces of gear which either deserve more attention or which bring to mind generally little-known facts.

I cannot overemphasize the necessity of thoroughly testing out newly acquired equipment on short, close-to-home trips before venturing on longer, more demanding outings. Then you will know what needs to be changed, improved, or returned for refund, and you will spare yourself troubles on longer trips to the middle of nowhere. You may not need to test the chocolate cake bought on special in a supermarket, but breaking in new boots is surely a must.

Clothing

Underwear should be very light, thin, and made of either polypropylene or wool. Angora wool is the most comfortable but also the most expensive. Polypropylene

A snack break in New Zealand. Evening clouds hide the Tasman Sea, otherwise visible from this Pioneer Hut area.

underwear is extremely light, quickly wicks perspiration away from your skin, doesn't absorb moisture, and insulates well. Cotton should never be used, since it doesn't insulate when wet and doesn't dry out easily. Make sure that the top half of the underwear (as well as shirts and sweaters) is long enough to prevent an exposed back when you bend over. It should reach below your crotch.

The next layer—shirt, sweater, and pants—can be made of wool or, even better, synthetic pile. Pile is warmer and lighter than wool, absorbs almost no water, and dries more quickly. For very cold and dry climates, down clothing is still unsurpassed, its high price easily offset by its long life and comfort. For wet climates only synthetic-insulated or wool clothing should be used.

Vests deserve special mention. They are one of the most

efficient garments, feeling surprisingly warm considering their simplicity and low weight and bulk.

A pile or wool balaclava is the best head and neck protection. Wools other than Angora may be itchy, and you may wish to wear a thin silk balaclava beneath. I strongly recommend a pile balaclava, rather than a conventional ski hat. A headband is excellent ear protection for the not-so-cold days.

A light face mask of aluminized fabrics, thin insulation, or a waterproof fabric like Gore-Tex is great for very windy storms or extreme cold. To be honest, I don't wear mine often, but I can't imagine surviving some of the bad storms I have encountered without one. Even with my balaclava and parka hood, my face would have been frostbitten. This item is so small and light, it has its permanent place in my pack.

A windshirt and windpants of uncoated, tightly woven nylon are really a must on the clothing list. They are extremely light; and they dry quickly, increase the warmth tremendously, and shed dry snow. On warmer days they can be worn directly over light underwear or with nothing under them at all. Check their windproofness by holding the fabric up to a light to check the tightness of the weave. I use them most of the time and save my much more expensive Gore-Tex pants and parka for the worst weather only. Some waterproof materials such as the early Gore-Tex garments offer excellent wind and water protection, but they have to be kept very clean to prevent leakage.

For my hands, I wear thin nylon gloves under pile or wool mittens and water-repellent cordura nylon overmitts. The thin gloves protect my hands from direct contact with icy metal when taking pictures or performing repairs and other chores in the cold. I add long cuffs to mine and also use them for sun protection when summer skiing. I have added wrist loop retainers to my overmitts, so I can take them off without fear of losing them. These wrist loops are available in some ski shops.

A clothing concept that is recently gaining popularity is the *vapor barrier system*, in which a waterproof shell garment is worn next to the skin, beneath the outer clothing. Such a garment, called a liner, very efficiently prevents evaporative heat loss and conserves a large amount of body heat. The perspiration rate and consequently dehydration

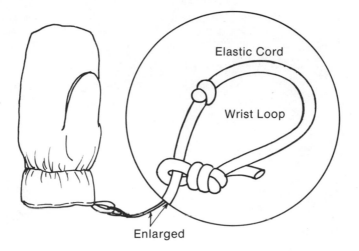

Enlarged

Wrist loop retainer for overmitts

is lowered. Vapor barriers also help keep your sleeping bag, parka, boots, and other clothing dry and clean. If you overheat while wearing a vapor barrier liner and start sweating, open it up and let the moisture evaporate. Most people don't like the clammy feeling of a waterproof fabric next to the skin. One solution is to use the garment with polypropylene underwear and socks that wick moisture away from the skin.

Vapor barrier liners can be bought commercially. But for feet and hands, ordinary plastic bread bags are more than adequate substitutes. In an emergency, wrapping a victim in large garbage bags, then in other layers of insulation, will increase his warmth.

Warm Feet

There are some time-proven methods to ensure warm feet. In extremely cold conditions, cover your inner socks with plastic bags, then add the outer thick socks, and cover them (or your boots) with another plastic bag. Old socks pulled over your boots are good too.

You might be amazed how much plain plastic bread bags worn outside the boots will increase warmth. Since the

bags rip easily, I always use them under ordinary over-boots. They are especially helpful in wet spring snow.

If your wool socks feel itchy, wear thin synthetic (Orlon, polypropylene) inner socks. Polypropylene socks are very comfortable and wick moisture away, which results in a dry, warm feeling.

Probably the best insoles are made of neoprene (wet-suit) fabric. They are excellent insulators, feel very soft under your feet, and prevent blisters. You can further in-crease warmth and comfort by placing thin, washable wool felt insoles on top of them. On longer trips, I carry two pairs of insoles. One pair is always drying out, along with an extra pair of socks, on my pack while I'm traveling.

Finally, over everything else come gaiters and overboots (see Chapter 1). This sort of leg protection is not only for snow. To get to skiable terrain in some parts of the world, it is necessary to walk through hostile flora, like the hook grass of Australasia. This nasty vegetable with its Velcro-like hooks grabs at the hair on your legs. I once found this dramatic account in a mountain hut's diary: "Monday. The going got so tough, I had to do something about it. I solved the problem by shaving the hair on my legs with a rusty tin can and set fire with methylated spiritus to the stubble. Tuesday. Came back to find an axe. Swarms of sandflies, feeding on my bleeding legs, prevented any progress. But I'll solve this problem, too. I'll chop my legs off." The les-son? Always wear your gaiters.

Are your feet still cold? Perhaps you should try double boots. Also keep in mind that the body extremities are the most vulnerable to heat loss, and you can prevent much of that loss by wearing extra mittens and a balaclava. When your torso and head are very warm, it takes only a short time for some of this extra warmth to flow down to your feet.

Another common cause of cold feet is wearing overly tight boots, which restrict circulation. Don't try to warm your feet by cramming on an extra pair of socks under your boots.

At night, don't leave your boots outside, but keep them inside a waterproof stuff sack between your sleeping bag and sleeping pad. They won't dry out, but at least they'll stay warm and supple.

(Left) Hut above the Murchison Glacier in New Zealand's Mount Cook National Park

Backpacks

For multi-day backcountry skiing trips, only large-capacity frameless or internal frame packs are practical. The traditional frame backpacks are too unstable for skiing; they lack the necessary flexibility and the body-hugging qualities. This doesn't mean that your frame pack is worthless; it may be totally adequate in gentle terrain, where you don't anticipate much turning. On short trips, any small pack will do; and on many trips, a waist pack will suffice.

There are many different models and sizes of frameless packs, including very large expedition packs. These packs hug the body very tightly, which prevents tipping or swaying and assures full control when skiing. They feel almost a part of your body. Because they are so simple, they are light with few parts to break. A high-quality internal frame pack is also a good choice.

Some friends of mine have found a way to improve their comfort when carrying great loads to a base camp. When

A body-hugging frameless pack (left) and an internal frame pack (right)

they head into the backcountry, they attach each pack to a frame with webbing and grommets. Then when they go on day trips with the packs, the detachable frames stay in camp along with the extra supplies.

Careful packing is essential for optimum performance and comfort. Concentrate the heavy items close to the spine to achieve lateral symmetry. If necessary, move the center of gravity lower or higher to find your own optimum level of stability and comfort.

For waterproofness, I always keep my sleeping bag, clothing, and other vulnerable items in large garbage bags inside stuff sacks. There is no such thing as a 100 percent waterproof pack or stuff sack. When I anticipate wet snow or rain, two more bags go over my entire pack. Waterproof pack covers are also available commercially.

A few straps and elastic loops strategically attached to the pack make it easy and convenient to fasten mittens, balaclava, and other items frequently put on and taken off.

When buying a pack, try out as many different kinds as you can, fully loaded. Judge their comfort and stability by walking around and simulating skiing movements such as poling, sudden jumps, and falls. Make sure your shoulders don't carry too much weight; rather, let your hips bear the load. Look for double or triple stitching in stress areas, a quick-release buckle, and a high overall quality.

Eye and Skin Protection

Sunglasses and goggles should be of the best quality. Buying cheap brands only invites trouble.

Sunglasses should have side shields for glare protection and a backstrap to prevent loss. Ordinary elastic holders for glasses are not reliable and may break. It is better to drill two holes in the frames at the temples and fasten a strong elastic band there. The best frames are made of unbreakable plastic, and the lenses must be impact resistant. They should block harmful ultraviolet and infrared rays.

Some lenses may look dark, but will allow injurious rays through. Beware of the many cheap imitations of well-known mountaineering glasses. They distort vision, fall apart after a short time and give very poor eye protection. In less than extreme conditions, photochromatic lenses, which darken in bright light and change to almost clear in low light conditions, are a good choice.

The best goggles are the large, polarizing, double-lens type. Such all-weather lenses give good definition in the low flat light of blizzards, yet protect the eyes reasonably well from bright light. If the sun is very bright though, good sunglasses are necessary to prevent snow blindness. Accordingly, carry both goggles and sunglasses. Make sure that the goggle lens is antifog coated. The coating will lose its properties after awhile, but it can easily be replaced with an antifog cloth, stick, or lotion.

The sun at high elevations is extremely intense, especially in spring and summer. Reflection off the snow multiplies its potency. Only glacier-type sunscreens should be used. Check that yours contains PABA (para-aminobenzoic acid, the best sunburn preventative). Be sure its SPF (Sun Protection Factor) is at least eight, which means the product provides eight times your personal, natural sunburn protection; with it you should be able to stay in the sun eight times longer than without it.

If you have sun-sensitive skin or are going to ski in extremely bright light, you should use products with higher SPFs. Currently the maximum available protection from burning is SPF 15. A note of caution: standard lip preparations function only as a moisturizer and have an effect in the snow-reflected sun equivalent to that of a cooking oil when frying a chicken. Use only time-proven lip-protecting compounds, as sold in good mountaineering stores.

In the summer, when the sun's rays are particularly intense, I protect my head with a white baseball hat with white mosquito netting and two holes for my eyes. I might look spooky to others, but at least I am well protected.

Light and Heat

A headlamp is very useful for night skiing or night chores and in the case of emergency or rescue. When using a headlamp, remember that one large battery is more efficient than a few small ones. Lithium batteries have the longest life, although they are the most expensive initially. Alkaline batteries are the next best; and because of their low cost and availability, they are an excellent choice. Any battery's efficiency decreases rapidly with temperature drop, so carry yours close to your body. For example, at $-7°$ C (19°F) alkaline batteries provide only 15 percent of their normal power output. Also carry spare batteries and bulbs. If at all possible, use a headlamp that employs the same batteries as your avalanche transceiver. The switch must be of a type that cannot accidentally be turned on.

A candle is an important accessory for snow cave and igloo living, since it warms as well as lights a snow shelter. Candles are also handy for starting an emergency fire.

An adjustable catalytic white gas handwarmer is an amazing source of long-lasting heat and will run a whole night at maximum heat output. It can be kept in your sleeping bag on very cold nights or placed inside your boots to dry them.

13. CAMP AND COMMUNITY EQUIPMENT

The previous chapter emphasized personal equipment necessary for all trips, including short outings. Longer overnight trips add to the list, primarily in the form of camping gear and group equipment.

Sleeping Bags

A good bag is slim, mummy shaped, hooded, with the highest possible loft-to-weight ratio, and is the shortest length practical for your height. When choosing a bag, rent or borrow different models and test them out. In a shop, crawl inside to check the comfort and size. Be sure you can draw the hood completely around your head and shoulders without compressing the foot section. Taffeta is a better outer shell than ripstop nylon. A Gore-Tex shell is even more desirable, since it will keep out the moisture from outside and will increase the bag's insulation value. But this material will add extra expense to the cost of the bag and must be kept clean to retain its waterproofing qualities.

Down is the best choice for sleeping bags for very cold dry climates. Fiberfill sleeping bags are better and sometimes lifesaving for wet country and for camping in snow shelters. In the latter, you need only a very light bag, since $0°$ C ($32°$ F) temperatures are typical in a cave or igloo.

A lightweight liner will help keep your bag clean and also make it slightly warmer. Waterproof vapor barrier bag liners are becoming popular. For extra warmth put plastic bags over your feet underneath your socks, then slide the foot part of your sleeping bag into your empty pack. For super-toasty feet, wear down socks. You can also hug your catalytic handwarmer, if there is nobody around willing to hug you.

To prevent moisture condensation caused by your breathing, keep your head out of the bag; for head warmth wear a headband, balaclava, or face mask. You can increase the thickness of your bag by fastening a light down or synthetic parka on the top by means of strategically placed Velcro tabs or cord ties.

The only way to assure your bag will stay dry in your pack is to put it inside a large polyethylene trash bag, then squeeze it into a coated nylon stuff sack. In the long run, any sleeping bag will be less damaged by rolling than by stuffing it into its stuff sack.

When it comes to cleaning sleeping bags, you have two choices. You can wash them by hand or in a large front-loading washer, using a mild soap or a special soap for down clothing. When washing synthetic-filled bags, fasten a safety pin through the inner and the outer shells every 30 cm over its entire length to prevent shifting of the fill. You can also dry-clean down, but not synthetic-filled bags. Be sure the cleaner uses petroleum-based cleaning agent, such as Stoddard Solvent.

Sleeping Pads

Beneath the bag goes a light closed-cell foam pad, of at least 10 mm thickness. Many experienced mountaineers prefer thicker 20 mm pads for a warm sleep uninterrupted by chill. The extra weight is well worth it, since thin pads are cold no matter how good your bag is.

Seldom is there enough space in a pack to squeeze in the pad. Lashing it on the outside of the pack is the usual solution, so you can glue two bands of coated nylon fabric to two corners of the pad, burn holes through them, and attach lashing cords.

The best foam is EVA (ethyl-vinyl-acetate), which insulates well and resists wear; polyethylene foam is lighter, but less durable.

Stoves and Cooking

For serious mountaineering, pump-type stoves should be used. There are only a few on the market worth considering. Assess your cooking needs and weight requirements, compare brands and prices, and choose the stove which is best for you.

My favorite fuel is kerosene—inexpensive, available worldwide, efficient, and much safer than other fuels. That it may be smelly or dirty should be of concern only if you are untidy and can't organize your cooking. Then use white gas. As an alternative, use deodorized kerosene. Attach permanently a few sheets of aluminum foil and a small closed-cell foam pad under the stove for increased efficiency and to prevent it from sinking into the snow.

For two persons, one large aluminum pot and a small pan (preferably Teflon coated), a small plastic spatula, a pot lifter, and for each person, a spoon and a plastic measuring cup are sufficient. For group cooking on long high-altitude trips, a pressure cooker is invaluable. Its extra weight is easily offset by the fuel and time savings.

Food is best packed in doubled plastic bread bags which are closed with a simple loose knot and put in a large nylon stuff sack. To save time and fuel, soak your dehydrated breakfasts overnight and your dinner while out skiing during the day.

"Living off the land," feasible in the summer, is unthinkable above the snowline. At most, you may be able to make rose hips or pine needle tea or eucalyptus tea when in Australia. Come prepared with adequate rations for each person per day. When figuring food amounts, make sure to account for the extra calories that will be burned up during each day's skiing. By the way, don't eat the carrots that fall from the sky in New Zealand. Saturated with poisons, they are dropped from airplanes to fight the rabbit plague.

There is one food that deserves your attention — sprouts. According to many nutritionists, they are the most complete food available. Sprouts are childishly simple to grow, inexpensive, and fresher than anything you can buy. You can sprout a variety of beans and seeds — sunflower, mung, lentil, sesame, alfalfa, wheat, fenugreek, radish, and many others — even while you are camping in the snow. Sprouts are not the lightest of foods, but can be an extremely valuable and tasty addition to a dehydrated food diet.

I have done some experimenting with the use of sunshine for cooking and melting snow. The sunshine falling annually on U.S. roads alone has twice the energy of all the fossil fuels burnt each year in the entire world. Just a microscopic chunk of it would make everyone in the backcountry happy.

Looking for a snow bridge over swollen Gore Creek, Colorado

With elaborate solar collectors, it is possible to generate temperatures as high as 3500° C (6332° F). Cost and weight make most collectors impractical for camping, but there are a few designs that show some promise. The parabolic reflector, a foldable umbrella-type cooker (weight 1 kg), is probably the most practical on short trips. The Fresnel lens focusing collector, a thin, light piece of plastic with molded-in concentric steps like a clear LP record, may be even better for the backcountry. To use a Fresnel lens as a cooker, mount three evenly spaced light aluminum wire legs on the thinnest and lightest lens available, at least 25 cm diameter. Blacken your pot and lid with soot, paint, or other coating before placing over the lens. Food can also be warmed in special plastic boilable pouches over the collected heat.

A blackened pot filled with your dinner and covered with a tight-fitting blackened lid will virtually cook by itself throughout a sunny day if left on insulation and wrapped in a clear plastic bag.

More information on solar cooking can be found in a book titled *People's Solar Sourcebook*, available from S.U.N., Box 306, Bascom, Ohio 44809. Fresnel lenses and other paraphernalia can be obtained through mail-order scientific, hobby, and school supply companies.

Water

On extended trips, most of the drinking and cooking water must be obtained by melting snow. A great deal of fuel can be saved by constructing a simple solar-powered "water machine." In its simplest form, it is a piece of black plastic with snow sprinkled on it. Any large dark object, such as a snow shovel, sled, or closed-cell foam pad, will work.

For a highly efficient water machine, I recommend placing snow in a large black garbage bag. To keep the snow spread out, stretch a sheet of plastic netting from an onion sack inside. Seal the bag, and insulate it from the snow beneath with a sleeping pad or with closed-cell foam sheets such as those used for packaging furniture. Position it away from wind and perpendicular to the sunrays. This will probably necessitate changing its location a few times during the day. Cover it tightly with a clear plastic sheet to create a greenhouse effect, and use a space blanket to reflect additional energy onto it. For assembling, use Mylar tape. This water machine works well even on hazy days, especially if the snow is wet or granular.

The mountain hut in some parts of the world is designed so the roof serves as a solar collector/water machine. The metal roof is oriented toward the sun and painted dark, so that any snow on it melts, running down a pipe and into a large container. The idea is good, but too often there is no water in the containers, only solid ice. The design would work better if the container were placed inside or if a flat black polyethylene box, tilted to receive maximum solar energy, were used as the water receptacle.

On a ski trip, water is of the utmost importance. The average mountaineer needs at least four liters of drinkable water to replenish his daily losses, higher than normal because of the dry air and activity, a point often underestimated by the inexperienced. Remember, you can

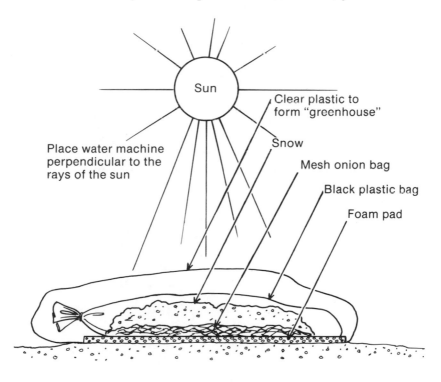

A water machine

survive many weeks without food, but the lack of water for a few days means death.

When you establish a base camp, start mass-producing water and store it in four-liter or larger plastic milk containers painted black. At night, they can sleep with you, or between sleeping bags. I drink my water mixed with a sport drink powder, which replaces lost minerals. I prefer to stuff myself with liquids at breakfast and lunch and even more so in the late afternoon, until my belly is on the verge of bursting. After that, I avoid large quantities of water, since I do not delight in crawling out from my cozy bag into a raging storm at 3 o'clock in the morning.

Even in the high country where there is no visible water, study the map carefully for creeks. When you can determine the *exact* location of one, dig. The fresh water may be under several meters of snow, but you will find it eventually.

Miscellaneous Items

Every party should carry a basic repair kit consisting of a spare basket, bailing wire, fiberglass packing tape, assorted screws, a spare bail (or spare parts for Alpine touring bindings), a small amount of quick epoxy with steel wool for filler, assorted tools, and a sewing kit.

An assortment of garbage bags in various sizes will find hundreds of uses, as waterproof overboots and overmittens, for trash, as waterproof stuff sacks, food sacks, wax sacks, emergency rain gear, and groundsheets. Conventional coated-nylon stuff bags are invaluable for keeping things organized. You may wish to label them for convenient in-camp access.

A stiff light hairbrush is unequaled for brushing snow off your equipment or tent floor to keep them dry.

One last pointer. For some people, the sound of a flapping tent or a snoring buddy can totally spoil a night's sleep. The solution—make yourself deaf by wearing earplugs, sold in pharmacies.

14. SLEDS

On longer trips, you will quickly discover the limited capabilities of both your pack and yourself as a carrier. The solution is simple: pull it instead of carrying it.

I have used sleds with great success on both short and long trips in Europe, America, and Australasia. On multi-day trips, you can haul gourmet foods like fresh vegetables, fruits, and sprouts or extra camera gear while getting the pack off your back and onto the sled. Sleds are invaluable if somebody has to be evacuated. They make you independent of food caches or air drops, so that very long, completely self-sufficient and self-contained expeditions are possible.

There are a few commercially available models of sleds on the market. Most of them are built solidly, which also means they are heavy and expensive. But I have found they work fantastically on long, demanding expeditions. You can build a good fiberglass sled yourself, but that takes time and skills.

For less demanding use the light, inexpensive plastic toboggans sold by many department stores will usually be adequate. While some models are weak, some are surprisingly indestructible.

To the front of the sled attach five meters of strong polypropylene rope and fasten the other end to a hip belt taken from any frame backpack. For safety, the belt should have a quick-release buckle. Attach a similar rope to the back of the sled, helpful in difficult conditions or when transporting a disabled skier.

Next attach a strong waterproof cover by riveting it along the front and sides of the sled. Install a zipper or cord closure at the rear of the cover. The cover should be made of a white fabric, or its contents may quickly reach the boiling point on warm sunny days.

The lack of pulling bars will of course cause some handling problems on descents, but it shouldn't be too much of a nuisance if you are an advanced skier. Just remember there is a beast chasing you down the slope. One day I was so engulfed in figure-eight wedelning on beautiful corn snow that I forgot about my sled. Needless to say, the sled came too close and bit off one of my heel locators.

If you don't want to be run over by your sled, you can improve the design in the following way. Instead of one five-meter rope, install two two-meter ropes in the front corners of the sled and slide aluminum tubing or light plastic slalom poles over them to make pulling bars. This slight modification will significantly improve your control of the sled.

When pulling a sled, wax your skis for maximum grip; or better yet, use skins. If possible, avoid long traverses, which are awkward and tiring. For long ascents, attach short lengths of climbing skin to the sled with strong tape, skin adhesive, or something similar. Now that strap-on skins have lost popularity, they can often be bought inexpensively at ski swaps.

For effortless downhilling, hot-wax the sled bottom and sides by melting a soft Alpine wax and applying it with a natural-hair paintbrush. If possible, run an iron (set on "wool") over the wax to increase impregnation, then leave it upside down in a very warm place overnight. In the morning, scrape off all but the wax impregnated in the sled

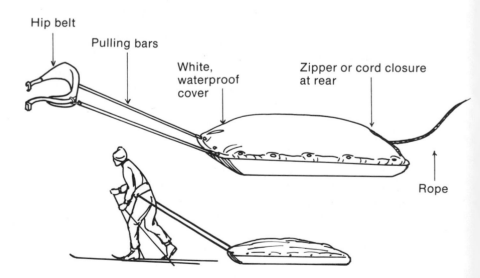

A sled for transporting gear

Naomi Yager dragging supplies for an eight-day expedition in Colorado's Gore Range

material. Repeat the procedure for best results. Keep in mind that hot-waxing gives by far the best long-lasting effect.

There are some situations where sleds are not practical—deep snow, steep terrain, tight trees, and the like. Sleds are most useful in easy rolling terrain, for transporting a lot of gear up to a base camp, or when traveling for weeks and weeks.

As with any other piece of new equipment, test the sled out on a short but demanding trip, so you won't encounter any disappointing surprises out in the wilderness.

15. SHELTER

Many American mountaineers look with envy at the extensive European hut systems. Countries like Norway, Australia, and Switzerland offer mountain huts that make a mountaineer's life quite comfortable. In a long nasty storm, such huts feel like heaven, especially if there are some good books, a guitar, and other skiers to share stories with.

There are plans to develop such systems in North America, but there are pros and cons to the idea. On one hand, huts are comfortable and provide a blessed shelter in an emergency or during a long wet storm. On the other hand, huts are frequently abused. I've been to many mountain huts in Europe, North America, Australia, and New

The Seaman's Hut in Australia's Snowy Mountains

Zealand, but have rarely found them clean and without the "signatures" of vandals. The Norwegian huts operating on an honor basis were in the best shape. The skier/climber borrows the keys from the managing body and, if necessary, can take food from open shelves and leave payment in the hut's cash box. I am afraid to say that such a system wouldn't work outside of Scandinavia.

Huts can also generate another problem. People may venture into the mountains unprepared, without even the basic essentials of emergency gear, presuming there will be blankets, food, stoves, and other equipment waiting in a hut.

Still I am not against huts. I couldn't imagine, for example, having a good time in a collapsing snow shelter or a leaking tent during a week-long Australian rain and hail storm.

Huts in the New Zealand Alps are very much appreciated by both "Kiwis" and foreign mountaineers. Due to the famous Kiwi tidiness, it is not surprising to find these shelters in good shape.

An exotic part of many New Zealand huts is a local bird, the Kea, a mountain parrot the size of a seagull. The Kea is extremely inquisitive and playful, and it loves to slide down hut roofs like a tobogganing child. Its curiosity can be damaging. Attracted by anything new and shining, the Keas often scratch cars with their strong claws and strip the window sealing and windshield wipers with their large beaks. Leaving any gear unattended is a grave mistake; upon return, you may find sleeping bags, food, and packs meticulously torn apart, as though visited by a grizzly bear. Keas are known even to kill a sheep for the gourmet feast of its neck fat. But you would never fear those cute-looking feathered birds if not warned. On a few occasions, shepherds have heard the birds screaming a sound like a mewing cat, a whistle, a chuckle, and a suppressed scream combined, as they joyfully ripped everything apart inside a locked hut. How did they get there? Through the chimney, of course.

Snow Shelters

Mountain huts are much too civilized for some. The option is either a tent or a snow shelter. Of the two, I personally like to use caves and igloos as much as possible.

A shelter built of snow is absolutely windproof and very warm, usually around 0° C (32° F) regardless of any blizzard outside. The exception is in the Arctic, where the temperature of the snow may be as low as −20° C (−4° F), making a really cold shelter until it's warmed up by your suffering body.

The fastest and easiest shelter to build is a snow cave. In favorable conditions one person with a good shovel can dig a small cave and be completely protected from the elements in as little as 20 minutes. A large palace-like cave shouldn't take longer than an hour, contrary to the common opinion of those who have never built one. However, ice layers in the snow, common in some climates, may slow or even prevent digging a cave.

The best building site for a cave is a small drift with a steep front wall. Naturally, stay away from avalanche slopes or cornices likely to break off. Wear waterproof but

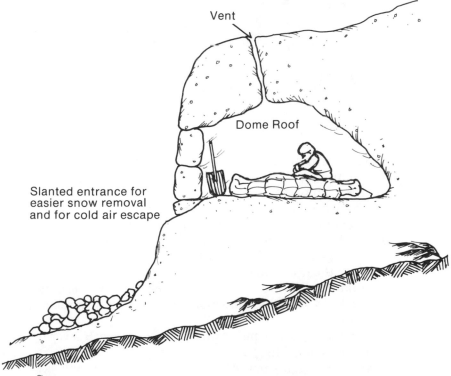

Vent

Dome Roof

Slanted entrance for easier snow removal and for cold air escape

Snow cave

Night life, snow cave style

not very warm clothing to avoid overheating and sweating while building the shelter. Wear wool or preferably pile mittens with overmitts. Even better, try thin wool gloves under surgeon's gloves. Make the entrance reasonably large for easier work, and later cover it in with large snow blocks. As you dig into the slope, throw the snow chunks onto a large garbage bag, which serves as a slide sending them out the door and down the hill.

Unlike an igloo, a cave may always be considerably expanded to include a kitchen, dining room, bedroom, whatever.

A long windy storm may cover the entrance with several meters of snow. There is not much you can do about it except keep digging out. Always store the shovels and ski poles inside, and mark the cave location when going away from camp. Even on clear days, a cave might not be easily found without some kind of external marker.

An igloo is a more elaborate and time-consuming structure to build. It takes two trained people at least 1 hour 15 minutes to construct one, although Eskimos can accomplish the task in half that time.

The first step in building an igloo is to pack down a flat area and let it sit for about 15-30 minutes. This hardening of the snow is called sintering. For the actual construction, you will need a shovel; a snow saw is highly recommended for cutting the snow blocks.

The inside diameter for two people should be at least 2 m. Cut the blocks as large as possible, at least $80 \times 40 \times 20$ cm. The size will vary depending on the cohesiveness and density of the snow. It's a good idea to permanently mark a scale on your snow saw and shovel to help you cut even blocks.

Erect a circle of blocks, then cut a diagonal ramp across three or four blocks to establish a spiral. Now place additional blocks, tilted inward, along the ramp and around the circle. Continue the spiral until you form a dome.

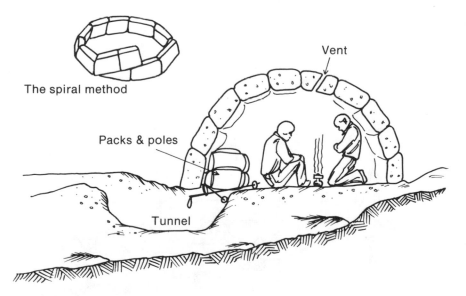

The spiral method

Vent

Packs & poles

Tunnel

Constructing an igloo

After the dome is closed, dig an entrance tunnel oriented perpendicular to the wind direction to minimize drifting into the tunnel. Finally pack all the gaps with loose snow, and smooth the outside and inside walls.

These basic instructions should suffice even for beginners. Try to avoid the most common mistakes—too large a diameter, uneven blocks, not enough inward lean (which results in a skyscraper igloo requiring a tall ladder to finish), and not allowing enough time for the packed snow to harden.

Any shelter will benefit from an airtrap entrance tunnel, built lower than the floor of the shelter itself. The warm air rises into the living compartment while the cold air settles into the tunnel. Include a vent in the roof to allow the air to circulate, and if you're using a stove, to ensure against carbon monoxide poisoning.

Very strong winds can erode an igloo, so build a protective snow wall on the windward side, and if necessary add another shell of blocks. Strengthening the igloo is extremely important in climates with warm winds and rains.

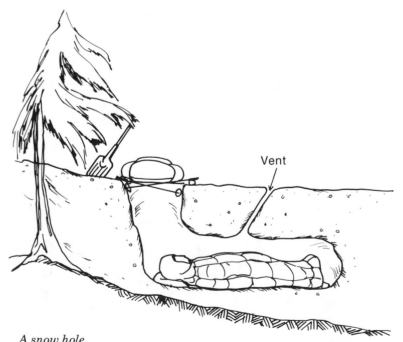

Vent

A snow hole

Nothing is more frustrating and dangerous than having your igloo collapse at midnight during a rainstorm. In rainy climates, it is safer to use a cave or tent.

After use, an igloo ices up inside, becoming much stronger and also making ventilation more critical. Icy walls conduct sound better than packed snow, and such an igloo is quite noisy. You can often hear the storm outside. Still, it is very peaceful compared to a tent.

A variation of the igloo is the snow mound, built by throwing snow into a heap, letting it harden for at least one hour, then hollowing it out to form an igloo-like shelter. Some people leave packs and bulky gear in the center of the mound, then dig them out later.

Another snow shelter is the snow hole—a good choice if the terrain is flat and the snow is deep and so cohesion-less that blocks for an igloo are too weak. The ideal site is among trees, close to a trunk. Building time is about a half hour. Remember to provide a vent hole in the roof.

Snow Shelter Living

To prevent your gear from getting wet, cover the floor of your snow shelter with plastic sheets or garbage bags. Then spread the sleeping pads over them.

Seal the entrance to prevent snow from drifting in and to avoid sudden pressure variations caused by wind gusts. These pressure changes can be of such magnitude that an open igloo will literally jump up, as in an earthquake, a peculiar experience, however harmless.

Dripping water, especially on above 0° C (32° F) days, might be a problem. Smooth the ceiling of the snow shelter into an even dome so the water will run down the walls. Keep the door and vents open. When the igloo seems to be getting weak, add another shell of blocks.

The Eskimos, who deal with extreme cold, have many ingenious ways of staying warm. For example, they hang animal skins along their igloo walls to form a liner that drastically reduces the direct heat loss from their bodies to the cold snow. You can benefit from this idea also; use a tent fly, space blankets, or similar materials as the liner.

Your first extended skiing trip will probably reveal a basic universal truth. Backcountry skiers just can't afford clutter in their camps. What will be the consequences if

A foot of fresh, dry powder coats igloo in Colorado's Gore Range.

boiling soup spills on the maps, or your knife gets lost in the snow?

Every single piece of equipment must have a permanent place where it will be put back after every use. Everybody and everything must be organized, military fashion. It sounds dictatorial, doesn't it? Some will have to change messy habits or face irritated companions and, what's worse, inevitable disasters. Being tidy and organized is as important as knowing how to telemark.

In large groups, it is helpful to mark all personal items with the owner's name to avoid confusion. A rather original approach to gear identification was demonstrated by a member of one of our expeditions. He could always find his socks simply by sniffing around.

What can you do on those boring storm-bound days, when even answering Nature's call is a test of your toughness? First make the igloo deeper, or at least dig a deep hole in the middle, so one person can stand up. Believe me, being able to stand up and stretch is a sheer luxury. You can install a window made of a plastic bag or sheet of ice. Then perhaps it is time to study the maps, discuss the first aid book or "boil your billy and hit the pit," which in the Kiwi language is to eat and sleep.

16. AVALANCHES

The two most critical hazards in the winter environment are cold and avalanches. Of the two, avalanches pose the greatest danger, since avoiding them must be based on knowledge, rather than equipment. If you prize your life and those of your friends, by all means take a good avalanche course and study the subject. Check with your local sporting goods store to locate the avalanche school nearest you. There are some excellent books on mountain snowpack, avalanche phenomena, stability evaluation, and rescue, but they are no substitute for field training.

Avalanches begin most frequently on 30° to 45° slopes. They do, of course, happen also on other slopes. There was a tragic accident recorded in Japan, where a wet avalanche on a 10° slope killed several climbers. Remember also, it's the slope angle in the *starting* zone that's important. Once in motion, avalanches develop tremendous momentum; they can run across flats, climb the opposite slope of a valley, even break and push trees uphill.

For stability evaluation of a slope, it is necessary, among other things, to know its pitch. To measure the pitch from a map, draw a simple diagram like the one on the right. The angle, being the average pitch of the slope, can now be easily measured by any conventional method, or with the compass protractor.

To measure the pitch of the terrain itself, use a compass mounted on a clear base. The compass may require small modifications. For example, a second cord hole may have to be drilled in the upper corner. Or, simply hold the cord in that corner. Turn the bezel until B (which is the normal "Read bearing here" mark) is at 90°. Make a permanent mark on the compass plate at A where it shows 0°. Now, tilt the compass parallel to the slope and turn the bezel until the meridian lines are parallel to the cord (which serves as a plumb line) and the orienting arrow points up. The slope angle can be read directly at A.

Under questionable conditions, dig a snow pit with your snow shovel and analyze the strengths and weaknesses of the layered snowpack. A few tools will help. Run a knife down the wall of the pit, and look for differences in the layers' strengths and cohesiveness. Rough compacted surfaces are generally more stable than smooth crusty surfaces. Horizontally stroking the pit wall with a soft 3×3 cm brush, will bring out variations in the hardness of layers.

If there are some particular warning signs in the snowpack—cracks, sudden collapse of snow ("whoomp!"), and settling sounds—don't play hero; turn back or choose a safer route. Needless to say, signs of recent avalanche activity indicate extreme danger. Remember, even a small, harmless-looking slide will be a death trap in a narrow gully. Many people have been killed in surprisingly small slides, on the order of 20 meters long.

To me, deep powder skiing in trees is one of the most enjoyable parts of a trip. I like the trees for two reasons. The powder there is the best, untouched by wind, sun, and usually by other skiers. Second, the trees stabilize the snowpack to some degree. So I try to avoid open slopes, chutes, or bowls and prefer instead heavily forested slopes, except in late spring when it's more stable and the corn snow is predictable in the open areas.

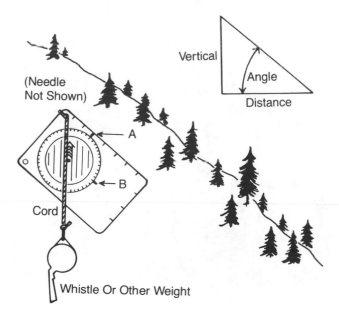

A compass with a transparent base can be used for measuring the steepness of a slope.

Avalanche danger is greatest in bowls and chutes (1), moderate in timber (2), and least on ridges away from cornices (3).

But the presence of trees on a slope can be deceiving. Scattered trees, perhaps more than five meters apart, don't give any protection, and avalanches can pass through them. As a well-known avalanche scientist puts it: "If the trees are far enough apart to allow comfortable skiing, the slope can avalanche." The problem is in defining "comfortable skiing." Some people require a half-kilometer wide bowl for only one turn, while others can turn on a dime.

There are also other factors to consider. It is usually warmer on tree-covered slopes, which—depending on prevailing conditions—may either weaken or strengthen the snowpack. Depth hoar, a cohesionless, ball-bearing-like layer, may form around tree trunks and rocks and make the snowpack weaker by decreasing the anchor effect. Depth hoar or "sugar snow" is responsible for the majority of avalanches in the Rockies.

The bigger and denser the trees, the better protection they offer; you can begin to feel pretty safe if you knock off a few branches and taste bark every other turn. It is very important to make sure the slope is covered with trees to the very top. Sometimes an open slope above can be a potential starting zone for avalanches that can easily squeeze through trees once in motion.

There is an arguable dilemma on whether or not to wear runaway straps in avalanche terrain. I prefer not to, although there are several factors to consider in making the decision. If a buried victim is wearing runaway straps, he may be found more quickly because a part of his ski may be visible on the surface, or because a rescuer's probe strikes a ski. Also, he will not lose his skis. However, the chance of an injury from a windmilling ski is increased. It is much more difficult to swim with the avalanche, and the skis may pull the victim into a deeper burial. Balancing these factors, I consider it safer to cross an avalanche slope without the straps.

Avalanche Transceivers

Transceivers are electronic devices that can both transmit and receive a beeping pulse signal. When skiers enter avalanche terrain, the beacons transmit a 2275 Hz pulse continuously. If someone becomes buried, the survivors switch to "receive" and home in on the pulse. If they know what they are doing, rescuers can locate the victim within five minutes and dig him out with shovels. This assures a reasonable chance of finding the skier alive.

There are three brands of transceivers available in the U.S. and Canada—the Ramer Echo, the Pieps, and the Skadi. They are compatible with each other. In Europe several models operate on a different frequency, so be careful when buying.

Statistics show that a buried person has less than a 50 percent chance of survival if not found within 30 minutes, although some researchers feel this estimate is too optimistic. I cannot overemphasize the need for extensive prior training in conducting transceiver searches. Your buried friend won't appreciate your reading the instructions and fiddling around while he is running short of oxygen.

Practice search techniques regularly. Work with a partner who buries his unit, then find it as quickly as possible. Working against a clock is a real incentive. A skilled ski patrolman may typically need five minutes to locate a victim, although the time depends largely on the size of the avalanche and other conditions. Practice at least once a month to remain proficient.

Avalanche statistics show that transceivers, used with snow shovels, offer by far the best chance of a live recovery in an avalanche accident. By no means, however, are they a substitute for avalanche knowledge and plain common sense. *Wearing a transceiver is not an invitation to ski avalanche terrain!*

Avalanche Cords

Avalanche cords are a relic and a poor choice of safety equipment. They are much less effective than transceivers and useless in trees, bushes, or rocky terrain. Still, an avalanche cord is better than nothing.

In theory, if you are buried, some part of the brightly colored cord trailing behind you will remain on the surface. Unfortunately, the cord may also be buried. To increase the chances of the cord's not being completely buried, attach a light, brightly painted plastic bottle to its end. The bottle will tend to float in the moving avalanche snow.

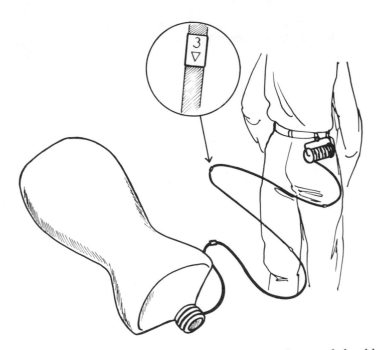

A reel for an avalanche cord, with inset showing how cord should be marked at regular intervals so that in an avalanche, distance to victim can be determined.

An avalanche cord tangles very easily, and winding and unwinding one quickly becomes a nuisance. I designed a simple reel that makes this chore effortless. I use a small plastic electric wire reel or an aluminum soft drink can squeezed tightly between the top and bottom to prevent the cord from sliding. After drilling two holes in the can, I insert an axle made of strong aluminum wire.

Shovels

Going on a ski trip with avalanche transceivers and no shovels is like taking a stove without fuel. It won't help your buried friend much if you find him "beeping" and possibly alive under two meters of snow, but have nothing to dig with. Avalanche debris is *very* hard, and speed is essential.

Fortunately, a shovel has many other uses. It can be used to build a shelter, such as an igloo or a snow cave. Digging a cave with a shovel may take 20 minutes, but with a cooking

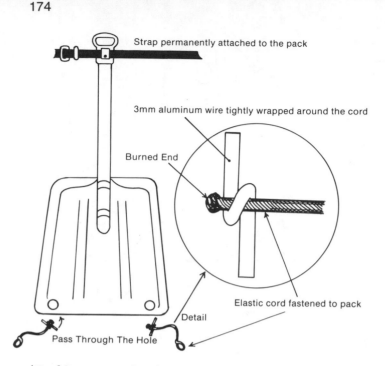

Strap permanently attached to the pack

3mm aluminum wire tightly wrapped around the cord

Burned End

Elastic cord fastened to pack

Detail

Pass Through The Hole

Attaching a snow shovel to a pack

pot it may not be ready before breakfast. A shovel is also valuable for getting to a creek buried under snow and building a cozy sheltered latrine.

I find one-piece shovels lighter, stronger, and more reliable than the collapsible models. Most one-piece shovels are never big enough to be a burden either on or inside a pack. Drill holes in the blade, and rig a method of attaching and removing it from your pack quickly with straps or elastic cord.

A D-shaped handle is the most comfortable to grip. The optimum blade size seems to be around 28×22 cm; smaller blades slow down the digging miserably.

The best shovels are made of aluminum or Lexan. To prevent the blade from icing up, heat it and rub on a film of soft (red) Alpine wax. An easier but less permanent procedure is to rub on liquid Alpine wax from a tube.

17. HYPOTHERMIA AND OTHER EMERGENCIES

A major threat in the backcountry is hypothermia, often rightly called "the killer of the unprepared." Frostbite is another potential danger. The well-prepared skier has the knowledge to prevent and, if necessary, to treat, these problems. And, just in case, he knows how to evacuate an incapacitated victim. The following information is only an introduction to these subjects. See Appendix B for in-depth books on mountaineering first aid and rescue.

Hypothermia

Hypothermia occurs when the temperature of the body's inner core drops below normal, because the body is losing more heat than it can produce. Typically it is the result of exhaustion and insufficient food and fluid intake in combination with wet clothing and cold weather.

Prevention is the best treatment, which means staying warm and dry. Here are some suggestions.

We often hear about the wind chill, the cooling effect of the wind on *bare* skin. The effect wind produces on bare skin is equivalent to a much lower temperature without the wind. For instance, a wind of 40 km/h at −1° C (30° F) cools bare skin the same as still air at −18°C (0°F). However, most people misinterpret this wind chill and make it seem much worse than it actually is. Skiers, eager to impress their friends, dramatically state, "Boy, the skiing was cold; the wind chill dropped to −45° C." What they forget is that this −45° C (−49° F) figure applies only to exposed skin. Naturally, if those skiers were mad enough to parade around naked, they could honestly say the skiing felt like −45° C. Even if they were wearing loosely woven clothing without any windproof outer shells, the wind would easily sneak through, seriously reducing the clothing's insulation value.

But wind speed will be reduced to almost zero at the insulation layer of a windproof shell; hence the wind's cooling effect will be small. You can prove this with a simple experiment. On a cold windy day, put on your warmest sweater and go outside. First stand on the wind-protected side of your house, then walk over to the windy side and notice how much colder it feels. Now put on a windshirt over the sweater and repeat the procedure. A tremendous improvement, isn't it?

A popular misconception connects the danger of exposure with low temperatures. In reality, most accidents occur between −1° C (30° F) and +10° C (50° F), because of the tremendous chilling effect of wet snow or rain, aggravated by the wind.

Wind can greatly reduce the effectiveness of any unprotected insulation. Water is an even greater enemy. The thermal conductivity of water is 240 times greater than that of calm air, making wet clothing nine times less efficient as an insulator than dry clothing. Humid air has less insulating value than dry. A given temperature in the humid climates of the coasts requires more clothing than in the Rocky Mountains.

Excessive perspiration also decreases the insulation value of your clothing. An experienced mountaineer may start a cold day wearing all of his clothing, but as soon as perspiration is around the corner, he opens zippers and removes his balaclava, hood, mittens, and other excess clothing. Of course he puts them back on during rest stops. A typical beginner, on the other hand, will suffer all day long, sweat dripping down his forehead. When he stops, his now wet clothing won't keep him warm.

Eat and drink frequently. Remember that carbohydrates supply quick energy, while proteins and fats are slower but last longer. "Scroggin" (in New Zealand) or "gorp" (in the United States)—a mixture of dried fruits, nuts, seeds, coconut, carob, and the like—is probably the best on-the-trail food, since it combines all energizers.

Get out of the wind and wetness, when conditions deteriorate. Set up your tent or build a snow shelter while you still have enough energy to do so. If you wait too long, this task may be too much for an exhausted body and mind. Immediately after stopping, put on extra clothing.

If trapped out in wet snow or rain, a couple of large garbage bags can save your life. Being totally wind and waterproof, they prevent heat loss by evaporation. Though perspiration will make the bags feel clammy inside, they will help your clothing keep you warm, and alive!

Symptoms of Hypothermia

The victim's temperature is the most important and reliable factor in determining the severity of the problem. Hence a hypothermia thermometer is an essential addition to your first aid kit. It should read from slightly below 25°C (77°F) to around 34°C (93°F), but preferably to 43.3°C (110°F) for measuring the temperature of the hot baths used to rewarm frostbite victims. In a pinch use the standard thermometer for measuring snow and air temperatures, but it isn't as good as a hypothermia thermometer.

The early symptoms of hypothermia may be shivering, slow slurred speech, and irrational actions. However, shivering may be involuntarily suppressed if the victim has had certain sleeping pills, sedatives, or alcohol; if he has hypoxia (insufficient oxygen in the blood at high altitudes); or if he is fatigued or is involved in heavy muscular activity (such as skiing or digging a snow cave). That's why it's important to take the body temperature even in the absence of shivering.

If the victim's temperature is down around 32°C (90°F), he has mild hypothermia. If severe hypothermia is suspected, the victim's temperature should be taken rectally. If this is not practical, a less accurate alternative is the oral measurement.

At 29°C to 32°C (84°F to 90°F), the victim will not be able to answer simple questions, such as "who are you," "where are we," or "what day is this." He may also demonstrate other forms of confusion, as well as drowsiness.

At 25°C to 29°C (77°F to 84°F), the victim will become unconscious or be very difficult to rouse.

At 25°C (77°F) and below, the victim will have no discernable pulse or respiration; he will *appear* dead.

Treatment

Get the victim into a shelter as fast as possible and remove all wet clothing. With cases of mild hypothermia, supply heat, preferably by placing the victim with a healthy person inside a cocoon made of sleeping bags and clothing. Both people should be stripped, since skin-to-skin heat exchange is the most effective warming method.

Make sure the treatment is immediate; if not, the rapid deterioration of the victim's condition may lead to death within a few hours.

For severe hypothermia, be very gentle when carrying the victim; avoid jarring. Do not let him exert himself by using his arms or legs. Apply hot compresses, hot towels, or any other available external heat source to the head, neck, and trunk, especially to the sides of the chest and the groins. These are the areas that are least insulated with body tissue. Even if the victim is breathing, you can add more heat to the body core by assisting ventilation with mouth-to-mouth breathing.

Do not try rewarming the extremities or giving hot liquids, since these will increase the blood flow; the blood from the extremities will then rush to the warmer core and cool it further. Rehydration is important, but stick to liquids that are no warmer or cooler than body temperature. Don't give alcoholic beverages as they dilate the blood vessels in the skin and result in more heat loss.

The treatment of the severe hypothermia victim is difficult and often unsuccessful. However, don't assume that a cold and seemingly dead person is beyond hope. Transport him very gently to a medical facility. If the victim is unconscious, avoid any sudden movement during transportation; cold hearts are so sensitive that the trauma may induce a fatal heartbeat disorder.

Frostbite

Prevention again is the key word. Since fingers and toes are the parts most vulnerable to frostbite, use warm mittens (and spares) with liner gloves; boots with sufficient insulation (two pairs of socks, closed-cell insoles, overboots, boot liners, or vapor barrier liners) will keep the feet warm.

If your arms feel cold, swing them. To warm up the feet, put on extra clothing and a balaclava. Be sure to eat and drink regularly. Don't smoke as nicotine constricts the blood vessels and thus makes limbs more susceptible to frostbite because of decreased blood flow there.

On cold windy days watch out for white (frostbitten) spots on each others' faces. If spots do appear, rewarm the areas in a shelter with a bare hand. If, despite all efforts, your hands or feet stay cold, get into a shelter, and let a friend warm them in his armpits or on his belly.

Rapid rewarming in a water bath of 37°C to 43°C (99°F to 110°F) is best for severely frostbitten limbs. Subsequently the limb should be covered with a sterile dressing, and *must not* be used for any activity. This approach is usually not possible in the field, so it is better to let the victim ski out on frostbitten limbs to a medical facility.

Evacuations

Though all skiers hope they will never have to face the necessity of evacuating an injured companion, an accident can happen to anybody, anywhere. So, just in case, learn evacuation techniques, and practice them *before* you need them.

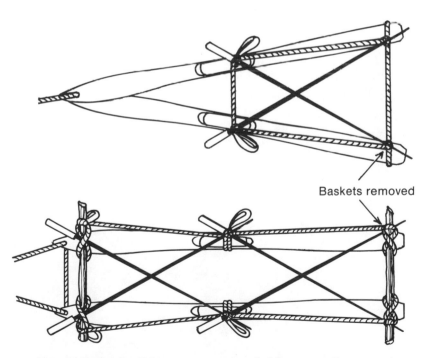

Baskets removed

Two methods of making an emergency sled for evacuations

It is simplified if you already have a sled in your party. Sleeping pads underneath and enough clothing over the victim will keep him warm and comfortable while you haul him out. But frequently, you will not have a sled with you.

There are many ways to make a sled out of skis, poles, packs, and straps. Holes predrilled in the tips and tails of your skis make the task much easier, so drill them today! Tree branches, ski poles, the internal frame from a pack, again predrilled with holes, can serve as cross braces. It is usually best to take the baskets off the ski poles. On top of this makeshift sled frame put packs and sleeping pads.

More than one pair of skis makes a more solid sled and decreases the drag. One person can pull the sled with a cord or with ski poles attached to the front, and one or two persons can control the rear by holding attached ropes. Skins will make ascending easier and descending safer.

Improvised sleds will not work in all situations. Use your imagination; it may be possible to evacuate the victim by other means. For example, you may be able to walk out or even ski by placing the victim on his skis and having him tightly hug a helper in front. Wrap the victim in a sleeping bag, pad, and tent, and pull him out. Or carry him in a large backpack after first cutting holes for his legs. Finally, check mountain huts which are often equipped with rescue toboggans.

18. WILDERNESS ETHICS

Most people venture into the backcountry to escape the rat race of civilization and to find unspoiled, clean mountains. Unfortunately not all outdoorsmen think that way.

Popular places like Mount McKinley, Mount Rainier, and many others will soon be invisible under the trash that mountaineers—yes, mountaineers like you and me—

Crooked Creek, Colorado

leave behind. Even drinking mountain water is becoming more dangerous to our health.

But is it really that difficult to observe a few simple rules?

• Pack it in, pack it out. Nothing should be left behind at a camp, except perhaps the buried ashes of burned paper. Do not burn foil or plastic bags; they are very light and can be reused many times.

• Do not wash yourself or your dishes in a stream or lake. Carry the wash water at least 100 meters from any water source.

• The latrine should also be at least 100 meters from any water source. Choose a spot that can't possibly become a camping place for someone else when the snow melts, and require everyone in the group to use this designated area. Whenever feasible, dig a hole through the snow and the top soil layer. Make sure that upon melting, the "yellow snow" will not run rapidly into a water source. Toilet paper should be burnt after use where fires are allowed, so pack a few matchboxes in with the toilet paper in a double plastic bag.

• Don't cut trees or branches, live or not. Use only camp stoves for heat and cooking, and sleeping pads rather than boughs for bedding.

• Collect the wax scrapings and pieces of containers you have used during your stay, and carry them back with you for proper disposal.

The basic rules of wilderness protection must be learned first, before anything else. It is sad to observe how some so-called mountain guides or instructors taking groups into the mountains don't even blink an eye when their unaware and uninformed customers damage the wilderness.

*Not all of skiing's pleasures are found on the slopes. Here a
touring party with an international flavor—an Austrian, a Swiss,
and a Pole—enjoy comradery in the Albina Hut, Australian Alps.*

Appendix A

EQUIPMENT CHECK LIST

This is a general and basic check list for trips of one or more days. It is to be adjusted according to the length of the trip, number of skiers, terrain, climate, and any other influencing factors.

Ski Gear
Skis with bindings and straps
Ski boots with neoprene insoles and wool felt insoles
Ski poles
Either climbing skins with a skin adhesive tube and a
    universal X-C wax (as a backup) *or* X-C waxes with cork
    and scraper
Universal Alpine wax (like the liquid P-tex wax in a tube)

For the Body
Long underwear
Shirt, sweater, vest
Storm parka
Long pants with suspenders
Windshirt and windpants
Raingear
Short wool socks (and extras)
Balaclava, face mask, headband
Baseball hat and mosquito net (for summer skiing)
Sunglasses *and* goggles with antifog cloth or stick
Gaiters and overboots
Liner gloves, mittens, overmitts (and extras of each)
Avalanche transceiver

In the Pack
Sleeping bag, liner, vapor barrier liner
Sleeping pad
Tent
Snow shovel and (for igloos) snow saw
Fiberfill booties with extra closed-cell foam insoles for
    warmth

Stove, fuel, pots, eating utensils
Food
Repair kit
10 meters of parachute-type nylon cord (at least 200 kg
    test)
First aid kit (including hypothermia thermometer)
Sunscreen and lip protector
Water bottle
Map and compass (with whistle, pencil, paper), map case
Handwarmer with fuel
Knife (with a screwdriver)
Toiletries (including toilet paper with matches for
    burning it), stiff hairbrush
Headlamp with spare batteries and bulbs
Candle and matches (waterproof)
Small and large garbage bags
Camera with extra batteries, accessories, and a fanny
    pack to hold it
Sled (for hauling the above) with skins and universal
    Alpine wax on it

Appendix B

FURTHER READING

Brady, Michael. *Cross-Country Ski Gear*. Seattle: The Mountaineers, 1979. A complete guide to skiing equipment construction, materials, and technology.

Kjellstrom, Bjorn. *Be Expert with Map and Compass*. New York: Scribner, 1976. An easy-to-follow guide for solving navigational problems using a topographical map and an orienteering compass.

LaChapelle, E.R. *The ABC of Avalanche Safety*. Seattle: The Mountaineers, 1978. The complete and acknowledged expert book on avalanches.

Mitchell, Dick. *Mountaineering First Aid*. 2nd ed. Seattle: The Mountaineers, 1975. A compact and excellent book for outdoors people about treating accidents and illnesses in remote areas.

Perla, R.I., and M. Martinelli, Jr. *Avalanche Handbook*. U.S. Department of Agriculture, Agriculture Handbook No. 489, 1976. A classic textbook on a wide range of avalanche aspects. A must for backcountry skiers.

Peters, Ed, editor. *Mountaineering: The Freedom of the Hills*. 4th ed. Seattle: The Mountaineers, 1982. A comprehensive text on mountaineering.

Sanders, R.J., Jr. *The Anatomy of Skiing*. New York: Vintage Books, 1979. A pocket-sized book describing Alpine skiing techniques very simply, but precisely.

Tejada-Flores, Lito. *Backcountry Skiing*. San Francisco: Sierra Club Books, 1981. A guide to skiing off the beaten track.

Wilkerson, James A., editor. *Medicine for Mountaineering*. Seattle: The Mountaineers, 1975. The complete reference on treating injuries in the backcountry.

Appendix C

CONVERTING FROM METRIC

1 mm = 0.04 in
1 cm = 0.39 in
1 m = 39.5 in = 3.28 ft = 1.09 yd
1 km = 0.62 mi

---

1 g = 0.04 oz
1 kg = 2.2 lb

---

1 l (liter) = 2.1 pt

°F = (°C × 9/5) + 32
°C = (°F − 32) × 5/9

Index

Accessories, Alpine touring, 127
Ascending, 130-33
Avalanches, 129-30, 134, 168-74
  cords, 172-73
  probe poles, 42
  transceivers, 171-77

Backpacks, 144-45
Base, ski, 34-35
  tuning, 44-46
Baskets, 41-42
Bindings, 128-29
  Alpine touring, 123-25
  cable, 123
  comparison of, 17
  mounting, 124
  non-plate, 123-24
  Nordic touring, 36-38
  plate, 123-24
Boots, 141-43
  Alpine touring, 120-23
  climbing, 120
  comparison of, 16
  double, 21-22, 121-22
  Nordic touring, 20-22
  waterproofing, 22

Cable bindings, 123
Camber, 25
  double, 26-28
  reverse, 26-28
Carving, 25-27, 78-80
Charleston, 104-105
Chutes, 128-35
Climbing plugs, 123, 131
Climbing skins, 17, 48-50, 131
  emergency, 50
Climbing wedges, 50-51
Clothing, 138-43
Cooking, 149-52
Cork, 47
Cost of equipment, 17
Cramponage, 103
Crampons, 14-16, 128, 131
Cross-over telemark, 100-101

Deep powder wedeln, 88-89

Descending, 133-35
Diagonal stride, 53-56
Double poling, 56-57, 70
Down unweighting, 65

Edges, ski, 35
  tuning, 45
Equipment
  Alpine touring, 120-27
  camp and community, 148-54
  comparison, 13-17
  Nordic touring, 20-43
  personal, 138-47
Ethics, wilderness, 181-82
Evacuations, 179-80
Eye protection, 145-46
Extreme skiing, 128-35

Falls, 108-117, 134-35
Firngleitern, 126
Flex, 27, 29
Food, 150
Frostbite, 178-79

Gaiters, 22-23, 143
Glissade, ski, 112-13
Goggles, 147

Harscheisen, 51, 127
Head lamps, 146-47
Heat, 146-47
Heel locators, 22, 38-39
Heel plates, 39-40
Huts, 159-60
Hypothermia, 175-78

Ice, 14
Ice axes, 16, 128, 131, 135
Igloo, 163-65
Impossible snow, 94

Kick, 53
Kick turn, 56-57

Lateral projection, 96-99
Leg retraction unweighting, 63-65
Longitudinal flex pattern, 28

"Mono" ski, 67-69, 79
MotiveAider, 122-23

Nordic Norm, 17

One ski turning, 99
Outrigger, 102, 109
Overboots, 22-24, 143
Overmitts, 140-41

Parallel turn, 73-77
Para-mark, 86-87
Personal equipment, 138-47
Pitch, terrain, 168
Plugs, climbing, 50-51, 123, 131
Poles, 40-43
    avalanche probe, 42
    self arrest, 42-43, 116-17,
    133, 135
Pretzel turn, 58

Races, telemark, 95-96
Recovering from a fall, 109-11
Repair kit, 154
Reverse telemark, 82-83
Royal christy, 103
Runaway straps, 37-38, 128-29, 171

Scraper, 47
Self arrest, 114-17, 134-35
    poles, 42-43, 133, 135
Shelters, 159-67
Shovels, 173-74
Shuffling, 52
Sidecut, 24-30
Sitz fall, 109
Skidding, 26-27
Skiing, extreme, 128-35
Skin protection, 145-46
Skins, climbing, 17, 48-50, 131
Skis
    Alpine touring, 125-27
    anatomy, 24
    base, 34-35
    comparison, 16
    design, 25-30
    edges, 35
    length, 30-32
    Nordic touring, 24-35
    short, 126-27
    tuning, 44-46

    waxable or waxless, 35
    weight, 35
    width, 32-33
Sleds, 155-58
    emergency, 179-80
Sleeping bags, 148-49
Sleeping pads, 149
Snow cave, 161-63
Snow hole, 164-65
Snow mound, 165
Snow shelters, 160-67
Solar energy, 150-54
Sprouts, 150
Step or jump telemark, 90-91
Stepping and skating turns, 77-78
Stoves, 149-52
Swing weight, 13-14

Telemark races, 95-96
Telemark turn, 66-73
    cross-over, 100-101
    reverse, 82-83
    step or jump, 90-91
    wedeln, 84-85
Terrain unweighting, 65
Terrain
    pitch, 168
    stability, 168-71
Tip drag wedeln, 106-107
Toe plates, 22
Torsional stiffness, 29
Traction, comparison, 17
Turning, 13-14
    and ski design, 25-30
Turns
    advanced, 81-107
    basic, 66-68
    carved, 25-27, 78-80
    one ski, 99
    parallel, 73-77
    stepping and skating, 77-78
    telemark, 66-73, 75-77
Two-pin bindings, 38

Unweighting, 61-65
Uphill skiing, 58-59
Up unweighting, 61-63

Vapor barrier system, 140-41
Vertical plane turn, 110-11

Walking, 59-60
Water, drinking, 152-54
Waterproofing, 22
Waxing, 17, 35, 46-48
Waxless skis, 35
Wedeln, 88-89
    telemark, 84-85

tip drag, 106-107
Wedges, 50-51
Weight of equipment, comparison,
    17
Wilderness ethics, 181-82
Wind chill, 175
Windshield wiper turn, 92-94

Other Mountaineers books you'll enjoy:

CROSS-COUNTRY SKIING, *2nd Edition,*
by Ned Gillette and John Dostal

A complete how-to book on cross-country skiing that
goes from the basics, on up to the use of cross-country
equipment on extended trips and expeditions. Loaded
with photos in instructional sequences. Authors have
directed several cross-country ski schools.

THE ABC OF AVALANCHE SAFETY, *2nd Edition,*
by Ed LaChapelle

How to spot and avoid potential avalanche areas,
(or survive, if caught), how to rescue avalanche victims.
Used by professional ski patrols, X-C skiers, snowshoers,
mountain climbers—anyone who ventures into the
mountains in winter. LaChapelle, former professor of
atmospheric sciences at the University of Washington,
works with the U.S. Forest Service on avalanche study
and control.

SNOWSHOEING, *by Gene Prater*

Designer, builder and veteran user of snowshoes, Prater
here explains how to select, use and care for snowshoes
for all types of terrain and snow conditions. Includes
techniques for everything from flatland walking to
tackling mountain slopes, from soggy Pacific Northwest
snows to the steep, ice conditions in the Northeast.

For complete listing of over 100 outdoor titles, write
The Mountaineers
306 Second Ave. W., Seattle, WA 98119